ONE-ON-ONE EVANGELISM
How to Make Friends for Jesus

Lee Moseley

High Bridge Books
Houston

CONTENTS

In Loving Dedication to...

My Initial "Table of Twelve"
(Matt Marcus, Tim Livingston, Jerry Crosby, Robby Buck, JP
Brooks, Jim Pearce, Buddy Hogan, Brian Ball, Jerry Batchelor,
Ken Jones, Tom Callahan, and Dave Markowitz)

In Deep Appreciation of the Ministries and Lives of...

Mike Baer, Walt Russell, and David Desforge
(Who helped move my life along this path)

Special Thanks to the Leaders and Members of...

Grace Community Church on Hilton Head Island, SC
Grace Evangelical Free Church in Lynchburg, VA
Fellowship Bible Church in Columbia, SC
Grace (PCA) Church in Fletcher, NC
(Who also helped move my life along this path)

FOREWORD

What does it take to make a difference in the life of another? How many men desire to have a life of significance and impact? Many wish, but few pursue. What is it that hinders men from taking the initiative to serve another man? Could it be that the way forward is foggy and unclear? The will to pursue others is there, but the means is elusive; thus, it's intimidating to connect.

Lee Moseley offers a way out of that fog. Based upon a life lived in pursuit of others, Lee walks men through the most practical of steps to engage other men for Kingdom impact. Looking into the life of Jesus and sharing personal lessons learned from his walks around the neighborhood, he provides those handles that allow men to bless other men. It is as profoundly simple as a walk, a story, and a friendship formed.

I've known Lee since 1978. He is the real deal. Everything written is personified in his life. One-on-One Ministries describes Lee. It is more than a program; it is a life lived under the hand of the Master, following His footsteps.

As you absorb the lessons from Lee's life, I trust that you will be inspired and equipped to make an impact, one person at a time.

Richest blessings,
Jim O'Neill
President, Association of Baptists for World Evangelization (ABWE)

INTRODUCTION

Jim Pearce sat across the table from me. I sat dumbfound-ed. How was I to answer his question? Jim had been a good friend for a long time. I was now in the throes of despair. Jim's question hit hard, right between the eyes. It entered deep into my heart.

"What are you now doing for the Kingdom?" he asked. It was a simple question, but profound.

"Well," I said as I finally responded, knocking off the cobwebs. "I guess you could say I meet with men regularly, either over a meal or cup of coffee. I just try to get to know them and become their friends. Eventually, God always seems to open a door that allows me into their hearts and lives, and I am usually able to help them in one way or another."

Jim then said, "Have you ever considered doing that as a ministry?"

"Can I do that, Jim?" I replied. I was quite shocked at even the thought.

"Sure," he said. "Bloom where you're planted."

I left that luncheon spellbound. "Start a ministry just befriending other men? Lord, is this what you would have me do?" The questions began to swirl.

On that day, God ignited a fire that soon became known as "One-on-One Ministries." I also had others encouraging me and God's Word speaking to my heart, showing me Jesus was constantly doing the same thing in his ministry.

It wasn't long before I was meeting individually with several men once a month and developing friendships with them.

Later, a purpose statement was developed, which is now the heartbeat of our ministry:

> *"To engage men in friendly one-on-one relationships with the gospel of Jesus Christ in order to help and strengthen their lives for the glory of God and His Kingdom."*

Later, our name was chosen, research was conducted, and an advisory group called the "Table of Twelve" was formed. Since then, One-on-One Ministries continues to develop through meetings with men from different sectors of society.

Such encounters have also led to many discussions in helping men of all ages and in various situations with issues involving such things as salvation, Christian growth, marriage, family, emotional upheaval, jobs, finances, counseling, advice, cross-cultural challenges, racial challenges, etc.

For example, Jake asked me to pray for his marriage.

David asked for prayer concerning his sick father.

Caleb shared about his divorce.

Dick discussed his involvement as a religious leader.

Carter, James, and Mike (all atheists) had ongoing talks with me about philosophy.

I have also entertained international businessmen from Vietnam, Germany, and India. All of them shared their lives with me over a meal and discussed the subject of faith.

Ralph, a local Christian businessman wrote,

> Thanks for thinking of me. You are so right about what a force we can be by simply reaching out to other men, one-at-a-time. I have been meeting with a friend one-on-one for two years now, weekly, and from this we have started our small men's group at church. Now we have 10-12 men trying to take our group to the next step reaching men one-on-one. Maybe we could have lunch soon and share some thoughts.

Since our start, One-on-One Ministries' monthly mailing list has grown from twelve people to hundreds of people, churches, and other organizations. I have even started speaking publicly on the subject of developing one-on-one relationships whenever possible.

The response to this type of ministry has been overwhelming. It is evident that God is using One-on-One Ministries to minister the gospel of His grace as we continue to meet so many men who have deep, personal needs.

The book you have before you is very simple. It tells us how we can become friends with others. It's a simple and easy presentation on how to develop relationships. In the process, you will quickly find yourself following in the footsteps of our Lord, who was known to be a "friend of sinners."

It is a relatively straightforward concept that anyone can apply, even people like you and me. My hope is that you may now read its contents and go with God's blessings as you become a friend to so many that need you.

CHAPTER ONE

JESUS WAS A FRIEND

"Now the tax collectors and sinners were all gathering around to hear him. But the Pharisees and the teachers of the law muttered, 'This man welcomes sinners and eats with them.'"
(Luke 15:1-2)

The prime objective of this book is to change your perspective on the subject of evangelism. In the process, I hope to make this type of outreach easy, fun, and exciting in your life. If you can just grasp the depth of one concept I will be trying to convey, and put it into action, then you will achieve all the fruit and labor of this material.

"And just what is that?" you ask.

It is very simple: "Learn to 'Be a Friend: One-on-One.'" I cannot state it any plainer than that. Simply put, "It is the art of learning to be another's friend."

"But it's not that simple," you say.

Most people think communicating the gospel is a complex matter. For a number of reasons, evangelism is often fraught with anxieties and fears. Most importantly, it scares many of us to death because a lot of models seem so intrusive and do not come from a natural outpouring of who we really are.

Therefore, because the subject of evangelism frightens us, we tend to want no part of it. When the topic arises, we become like Jonah and head for Nineveh. Or, we set out to attack others verbally like Balaam, whose approach lacked both love and direction from God.

In *Be a Friend: One-on-One*, I hope to give you, the reader, a new and different perspective. I want us to look at the life of Christ and observe a Biblical foundation that is both natural and enjoyable at the same time.

I also hope to show you how easy and loving it is to be someone's friend "to so fulfill the law of Christ" (Galatians 6:2). As we love others, we'll have fun in the process, working alongside our Lord and his people in the harvest fields of life. There's nothing like it at all!

As a result of reading this book, I hope that, one day, you'll look back and say, "I never dreamed it was so easy. There is nothing I like to do more than meet people and become their friends. Absolutely nothing!"

Now, as we engage this time together, I ask that you would pray and petition God to give you an open heart for what He has for you to receive. May my prayers and the prayers of many be with you at this time as you engage this all-important matter, and may our hearts be rekindled once again with the love of Jesus, who was known in his day to be a "friend to sinners."

CHANGING PERSPECTIVE

Four frogs hopped down an ole dirt road. Two were about 20 feet ahead of the other two when, suddenly, the first two fell into a deep hole.

When the other two frogs finally arrived at the top of the hole, they saw the two below trying to escape. They realized immediately that any pursuits to help were futile as the hole was very deep.

Soon, they began screaming and waving their little arms and legs saying, "Stop! Stop! You're only going to hurt yourselves! Stop!" But the little frogs continued to try and jump out of the hole in vain.

Finally, one stopped, curled up, and died. But the other one continued jumping.

The more the two at the top of the hole yelled, the more the other little frog kept jumping. Finally, despite all their pleas, he jumped out of the hole.

In their amazement, they came over to the little frog, got face to face with him, and asked, "How did you do it? How did you make it out of that hole?"

He replied, "Fellas, I am deaf, and I saw you two cheering for me. That was the motivation and encouragement I needed to be able jump out of the hole."

You see, one's perception worked for the bad while the other's worked for the good. How we perceive things does matter.

What is your perception when it comes to reaching others for Jesus? In many cases, our understanding of what has been modeled for us has dulled our senses. This is what One-on-One Ministries is trying to change in the lives of men. If we had to nail it down, our purpose statement would be: "To engage men in friendly one-on-one relationships with the gospel of Jesus Christ in order to help and

strengthen their lives for the Glory of God and His Kingdom."

So, how do we change our perception? To start, we
first must look at the life of Christ and observe the example
He passed to those around him. What did he do, and what
did he model?

We talk of Jesus often as being *Prophet, Priest,* and
King, but how often do we see him in the light of the gospels as being *Friend*? Throughout His life's ministry, Jesus
was known as just that: "a friend to sinners."

Take a concordance, and look up the word *friend* or
friends in the Gospels. It might surprise you just how many
times Jesus is seen as a friend or as calling others his
friends.

Look at all of the close relationships Jesus had and the
multitude of relational contacts he made. For instance, the
Seventy, Lazarus and his sisters, the Twelve Disciples,
Zacchaeus, the woman at the well, Nicodemus, the centuri-
on, John the Baptist, the demoniac, Salome, the boy with
the two fish and five loaves, Joseph of Arimathaea, and the
list could go on.

Have you ever seen evangelism in the light of "being a
friend?" Did you know that 85 percent of people surveyed
said the greatest influence in their coming to Christ was
through a relationship with another individual? If this is
true, our primary focus should be to teach others the art of
befriending. As we initiate these types of relationships, we
will be able to connect with people on a deeper level.

As Christians, we carry with us God's presence and
cannot help but to exude the light of Christ. This eventually

moves our friendships into natural conversations that progress into discussions about our Lord. Sometimes, God opens up these discussions rather quickly. At other times, they take long periods to get into the heart of another's life.

What I am saying is this: "Jesus' model of evangelism was often befriending others." This has become our theme at One-on-One Ministries: learning to "be a friend."

"Meeting others," I pondered. I was thinking about that when I spotted him. I was on my evening walk when he appeared out of nowhere.

"Hi," I said.

"Hey," he replied. "I see you walking everyday."

We introduced ourselves. His name was Joel. We walked together for a while and talked. I could tell he was mentally impaired.

Joel shared a little about himself and his faith in Christ. As we parted, I asked him if I could pray for him concerning anything in his life. I also asked if he would pray for me.

He told me he would and that he prayed for me when he saw me out walking the night before. Later, I thanked God for Joel.

That was such an encouragement to me. Joel and I are now friends. I ran into him again recently. Joel said he was still praying for me.

One evening, Jesus met a man. He was a religious leader by the name of Nicodemus. He had a few questions for our Lord (John 3).

Soon, we begin to see Nicodemus standing in defense of Christ before the religious leaders of his day (John 7:50-51).

What kind of impact did Jesus have on him that night? Apparently, it was a profound one.

Are we meeting others? We'll talk about this more later, but for now, let us keep in mind that Jesus was constantly befriending those he encountered.

The question is, "Are we?"

TELLING YOUR STORY

We all have a story to tell. We have all encountered various people through unique circumstances. Think for a few minutes of the places you have been and the things you have done. Now, think about some of the people you have met. Then, think about those around you that also have similar stories, just like you, to tell others who are willing to listen.

I live in Greenville, SC and grew up as the oldest of four children. While growing up, we lived in a unique area, filled with boys and girls. I still have some of those relationships to this day.

When I was 17, I joined the US Army and served Uncle Sam in both California and Korea. Some of the greatest times in my life were spent talking with friends at the motor pool or on the end of a barrack's bunk.

When I finished my military duty, it was off to college. There, a whole new arena opened. I met people who seemed to have my same focus in life. We studied together, played, laughed, cried, schemed, and envisioned our futures together.

Then, there were the three years between college and graduate school. I spent most of it at the beach, and there I became the president of a singles ministry. Again, I met people just like me. We all seemed to be unsure of where we were going, but we were having fun doing it together.

Finally, I met my wife, and life became meaningful. It was then back to school and seminary to get my master's degree. There, everyone seemed to be focused on the future. Many were newly married and having children like us.

At seminary, I met a professor named Walt Russell who helped to shift my approach to discipleship and evangelism. In a nutshell, Walt's challenge for discipleship was simply to surround yourself with friends and, together, grow unto Christ while sharing your lives with one another. It was a transforming experience that not only changed me but also my entire future ministry.

I could go on, but I'd like to ask, "Did you know that every person you meet has a story?" They all involve places, events, and people who have impacted their lives.

By the way, "What's your story?"

JESUS WAS A FRIEND

Do you believe Jesus desires to be a friend to you and to others? Have you ever studied the life of Christ to see what he spent most of his time doing?

Jesus was reaching out to those around him constantly. Think about it. Think about how he reached out to us and called us to himself. He was working constantly on our hearts even before we came to him. Have you ever thought about that? God was at work in our hearts, drawing us to himself, even before we realized he was reaching out to us. Now, he is calling us to the same. He is calling us to reach out and befriend those around us.

Who exactly are those around us that he wants us to meet and befriend? To help us answer this question, let's ask another one: "Who is God putting in our paths of life?"

"But, you don't understand," you may saying. "Some of the people that cross my path are much smarter than me."

Did Jesus' paths not encounter people like the rich young ruler or Nicodemus? These were apparently educated men of great stature?

"But, you don't understand. Some of the people that cross my path have some serious economic and sociological problems."

What about the lady that gave her last two mites or the woman at the well? Did not the heart of Jesus reach out to them?

"Yes, but, you don't understand. I work around some rotten people. I have to deal with their lying ways everyday."

How about the thief on the cross or Judas, who was a disciple of our Lord? I guess we could go on and on, but was not Jesus constantly befriending those who crossed his path in life? Was he not a friend to sinners everywhere he went?

Everyone is at a different place or stage in his or her lives. Some do not believe in God; others believe but have no active faith. Then, there are those who believe and live good, moral lives, yet they have no real relationship with Christ.

Others even talk the talk, but they do little to walk the walk. Yet, for some reason, God has placed all of these people in our paths.

It could be that you have already developed a relationship with them. It could be that they are a friend, relative, associate, neighbor, or just an acquaintance. Who knows? Yet, they keep crossing our paths.

Do we, like Jesus, desire to know those in our sphere of influence? Do we, like Jesus, desire to be their friend? Remember that Jesus was a friend to sinners.

A FRIEND TO OTHERS

Have you ever considered that Jesus is also about reaching those outside of our spheres of influence? Did he not tell his disciples that those who are with us are not against us? (Mark 9:40) And did he not also share with them that we would be witnesses all over the world? (Acts 1:8)

There are people close to us and far away in need of a friend. The question is, "Are we looking for them?"

Did you know there is a great difference between frogs and lizards? Frogs often sit on lily pads and wait for their daily meals. Lizards go out exploring in hopes of finding food.

Often, our evangelism is like that. We talk about it while we sit waiting for something to happen. We're a lot like the frogs. Instead, we should be more like the lizards. Life is a lot more exciting when we go hunting for those whom God has for us rather than just sitting and waiting for them to appear!

Did Jesus not also tell us to "Go?" (Mark 16:15) Did he not also tell us to go into the highways and hedges and compel them to come in order that his house might be full? (Luke 14:23)

Therefore, getting to know new and different people is our calling, but it is also an exciting adventure. It is one of vital importance that our Lord has called us to do.

Do we desire to know others who are in need to become their friends? If you are truly a Christian, I cannot help but believe the Spirit of God has also placed this in your heart as he has in mine.

As an added note, I have also found it very helpful to learn to be a good listener with those to whom we come in contact. The Apostle James once said, "Be swift to hear and slow to speak" (James 1:19). That just makes sense; doesn't it? If we are always talking, how in the world will we ever be able to learn about others? Therefore, whenever we encounter other individuals, try to listen and hear what they have to say.

I once noticed a man who had a book in his hand while standing in line for food. "What's your book about?" I asked.

Over the next few minutes, he told me all about his book, his life, and his philosophy for living. He was an avowed atheist. I showed an interest in wanting to hear more of what he had to say.

We met again a few days later in the same eating area. It wasn't long before we were meeting regularly. We soon became friends.

In time, he wanted to hear about Christ and Christianity. We had some long talks, and our friendship grew.

I often wonder, what would have happened if I showed no interest in him? Suppose I never listened to what he had to say that day when I asked him about his book? Where would our relationship be today?

PRACTICAL APPLICATION

Try listening. Ask someone out to lunch. Ask them questions about themselves. Try to hear what they have to say.

Do the same thing at home around the dinner table. Ask a few questions to get the ball rolling, and then just listen. It will amaze you what you might learn.

In our conferences, we split into groups of four people. These four people know little, if anything, about one another. Then, one-by-one, each person takes four minutes sharing about himself without anyone else saying a word. When the four minutes are up, the next person begins using the next four minutes to tell the story of his life. This goes on until all have shared four minutes about their life with the others. Everyone always tells us later how much he or she learned in those sixteen minutes of dialogue.

It is a practice you can use at business meetings, with your family or friends, at activities, etc. Just have people share from the time of their birth forward. Some will take only two minutes. If this happens, they can then share about their favorite hobbies, sporting events, movies, or anything they desire. Others will just be concluding with their moments in kindergarten when the time is over, but when their time is finished, it is finished. It is all part of getting to know those around you.

Remember that "Jesus was a friend to sinners." Now, let us go and do likewise!

CHAPTER TWO

BECOMING A FRIEND

"He that hath friends must show himself friendly,
And there is a friend that sticks closer than a brother."
Proverbs 18:24

I had just moved to Hilton Head Island, SC. My mother moved down there two years earlier to do art, but instead, she started a cleaning business out of the back of her car.

The time was now right for me. I was not sure about my future. It had not been long since I graduated from college, and helping Mom with her business sounded like a good idea. So, it was off to Hilton Head to sleep on a sofa and to enjoy my time at the beach.

Three months later, I was depressed and all alone. I'd go to work and then come home and watch TV until I fell asleep. All I could think about was, "Where is my life heading?"

I cried out to God, "I'm lonely Lord."

A few days later, I heard there used to be a singles group on Hilton Head, but it had disbanded. My loneliness crept in again.

Again, I found myself before his throne crying, "Lord, I'm lonely. What do I do?"

The book of *Proverbs* had often challenged me in the way I should go. That night, I was reading chapter 18 when I found my answer. Verse 24 simply states, "If you're going to have friends then get out there and be friendly toward others" (my paraphrase).

"Lord," I thought, "So you're saying if I will just get out there and reach out to other individuals, you will give me friends, and I won't be lonely anymore? Okay then, I will."

"And Lord," I prayed too, "If I do this, I'd like to be a part of the upstart of the singles ministry here again on Hilton Head and one day be its president."

So, that's what I prayed. Three months later, the singles ministry was back in full swing, and I was its President. Many young singles from all over Hilton Head Island were meeting at an event on Friday nights that we called, "Every Single Friday."

My life quickly went from loneliness to having more friends than I had time to meet. It was almost overwhelming. That's when I saw the principle of friendship evangelism taking place in my life on a large scale. I also saw that this calling was not only for me alone but also for all of God's people.

As we continue to engage this topic of "becoming a friend, one-on-one," I want to ask two questions:

(1) Are we befriending others?
(2) How are we to befriend others?

It's now time for us to look at a new perspective in developing friendships with those around us.

I once heard of a farmer visiting his banker. The two greeted one another and then sat down to talk.

"So, what brings you by today, Mr. Farmer?" asked the banker.

"Well Mr. Banker," responded the farmer, "I've come by to give you some good news and some bad news."

"Oh?" responded Mr. Banker. "Then, give me the bad news first."

"The bad news is, I can't pay my mortgage this year because our crop was so bad."

"Well, Mr. Farmer. That is some bad news."

"But that's not all, Mr. Banker. Most of my equipment is broken down, so I'm not going to be able to pay the equipment loan either."

"Yes sir, Mr. Farmer. That truly is bad news."

"Well, I hate to tell you this, Mr. Banker, but that's not the end of it. Because we had such a bad crop, and all my equipment is broken down, I've used up my equity on the farm and the line of credit I have with you. I can't pay those back either. I'm just broke, Mr. Banker! Flat broke!"

"Oh my, Mr. Farmer. This truly is disturbing news, but you also said you had some good news."

"That's right, Mr. Banker. I do. My good news is I'm still going to keep doing business with you."

Isn't that the way it is in life? We have an opportunity to see things from one perspective or another. How do you view life as it relates to developing friendships with others? Do you see it as something exciting, fun, and easy to do?

Or, do you see it as drudgery, hard, and something uncomfortable that you'd rather not do, but you feel you have to do?

It is my hope that God, through his Spirit, will change our perspective and make developing friendships one of the joys of our lives.

SENSITIVITY TO OTHERS

In our last chapter, we looked at the life of Jesus and those he encountered in ministry. I then encouraged you, in your sphere of influence, to reach out to those around you. I also encouraged you to consider reaching those you don't know who are also in desperate need of Christ.

As we move forward, I would like us to see that befriending others also starts with envisioning friendships as a reality in our lives while being sensitive to those we encounter. Do we see others in need of our Lord? The Bible says, "Where there is no vision, the people perish" (Proverbs 29:18). Do we see ourselves as instruments of God's love and grace? Do we see ourselves engaging others and becoming their friends?

All around us, people are hurting. They are struggling with numerous issues in their lives and have no one to talk with concerning their stresses and pains. They need someone to come alongside them to be nothing more than a friend.

"Where are they?" you ask. They are everywhere. Wherever you go, people are dealing with job issues, marital problems, family upheavals, bad health, the lack of money, relationship breakups, etc. More than anything in this world, they need a friend who will show them the love of Christ.

In his book, *Lifestyle Evangelism*, Joe Aldrich talks of envisioning God's Spirit at work, hovering over the places we spend most of our time. Aldrich encourages us to see the Holy Spirit working in our midst as he opens doors of opportunities to share our lives with those around us.

For instance, let's say you move into a neighborhood and believe God sent you there to be a part of his work in the lives of your neighbors. So, you start praying for God to open doors and, eventually, to make an impact for Christ.

One day, you meet Bill as he is raking his yard. The conversation moves from the neighborhood to things you both like to do outside of work. He tells you about some of his fishing ventures. You mention to Bill that you don't fish, but you've always wanted to learn.

Over time, Bill invites you to go fishing. You go, praying and watching God slowly develop this friendship. One day, while on the boat, Bill asks you about your Christianity. Now, you've never said anything about Christ up to this point, but Bill knows of your faith because the Spirit of God has put you in his path and has been working on him, causing Bill to see Christ in you. All you had to do was pray, be a friend, and wait for God to move on Bill's heart.

"Is that all?" you ask.

Yes, that's all there is to it!

If that is true, are we envisioning God at work in the lives of those around us? Do we show ourselves friendly toward others? Are we sensitive to them and their needs?

Jesus was. He was a friend to sinners. Constantly, he was showing himself to be friendly.

Mike was an investor. He helped me to coach a youth soccer team. Our kids grew up together. I always assumed he was a popular guy with a lot of friends. Every time we talked, I tried to show an interest in Mike. I'd ask him questions about himself, his business, his wife, and his family.

One day, the phone rang. It was Mike. He said, "Lee, could we meet for lunch? I'd like to talk with you about something."

"Sure," I said.

When we got together, Mike's eyes watered as he shared that his marriage and family were in shambles. At first, I was shocked. Then, Mike told me he was at the point of suicide and that I was his only friend.

Again, I was reminded that we should never assume anything about those with whom we come in contact. You see, people are people, and all people are struggling in one way or another. One preacher once put it like this: "Everyone is at one of three places in their lives. They are either suffering, have just gone through suffering, or they are getting ready to go through suffering."

Job stated it so well when he said, "As the sparks fly upward, man is born unto trouble" (Job 5:7). Later, Job says, "Man who is born of woman is of few days and many troubles" (Job 14:1). Everywhere we go and with everyone we encounter, we have to deal with people and their hardships. It is something we need to understand and envision while being sensitive as we engage others in our daily paths of life.

There is an old saying among hunters, "You can't hit a target if you're not aiming at it." How true! Yes, you might get lucky and strike the bull's eye, but for the most part, if you aren't aiming at it, you will never hit it.

Jesus told us plainly, "The fields are white unto harvest, but the laborers are few" (Luke 10:2). If we are ever to be a part of God's harvest, we must consider that we have to be laborers.

Are we envisioning this? Are we making it our aim and point of focus? Do we see God at work in those around us? Are we showing ourselves to be friendly?

Jesus did. He was known to be a friend to sinners.

BEING ALERT

I was out of college for the summer. Chuck visited our church. He was from across town, the rough section. His ways were intrusive. He smelled. No one wanted much to do with him, and he seemed to be avoided by all.

The Holy Spirit's conviction would not let me go. I approached Chuck, and we became friends. He liked basketball, so many days, we'd shoot hoops together and then grab a bite to eat.

One day after our game, I asked Chuck to come to my house for lunch. Mom fixed some hot dogs as we sat and talked at the table.

When Mom finally arrived with the food, she asked Chuck, "Are you a Christian, young man?"

"No, Mrs. Moseley," he replied. "I am not."

Mom then asked, "Would you like to know how to become a Christian, Chuck?"

"Yes, I would," he responded.

"Then you would not mind if Lee took you into the other room after lunch and showed you from the Bible how to become a Christian?"

"I'd like that," Chuck replied.

Thirty minutes later, Chuck had received Christ and his whole life began to change. Years later, I saw Chuck again, and I am happy to report he was still growing in his walk with Christ as his countenance radiated his service to our King.

God often places us in situations to meet others wherever they might be in their spiritual journey. Our call is to be attuned to what God is doing and when he is doing it. We are to look for opportunities to sow seeds of friendship whenever we can.

I was taking my evening walk in our neighborhood. I'd been praying that God would help me to reach out and get to know my neighbors. Then, I saw a man with only one arm trying to fold this huge tarp in his front yard.

I stopped, walked over, and said, "Let me help you."

Ten minutes later, I had formed a new relationship with Bill. After shaking his hand, I headed down the street and prayed for my new friend. I'm looking forward to seeing Bill again.

Do you see what I am saying? It is all about being alert to others and to what God is doing in their lives. That's what it's all about. It's learning to be sensitive to others' hurts and pains while finding out their needs and then reaching out to try and help them.

It could be as simple as helping someone move, cutting another's grass, clipping out a special newspaper article to pass on, writing a note, taking someone to the doctor, changing oil in their car, or watering a friend's plants. It's anything that calls for a need to be filled and then responding to it.

Are we being sensitive to those around us in order to show ourselves friendly?

I told a friend I would be in the countryside on Tuesday. He asked if I would stop by his family's old farmhouse and pick up the mail.

The next day, as I was standing at the mailbox, I saw a young man walking down this barren country road. I said, "Hello," and I asked him where he was headed. When he told me he was walking to town, five miles away, I offered him a ride.

When I told him I was a minister, he immediately opened up and started sharing his life. The pain this young man was experiencing was great. We ended up talking for thirty minutes and finally prayed together.

I truly believe opportunities will abound if we will only looking for them. Jesus was constantly engaging others throughout his daily life. Acts 10:38 tell us, "God anointed Jesus of Nazareth with the Holy Spirit and with power: who went about doing good, and healing all that were oppressed of the devil; for God was with him."

Are we also engaging others while being alert and attuned to their needs? If we look at the life of Christ, he was constantly doing this. He was always showing himself friendly while reaching out and entering into the lives of others.

I had been between churches for a year and a half. I was down. Why had God not opened a door for me to minister? Jim Pearce sat across from me at lunch that day. He is a dear brother and a trusted friend. I told him of my depression.

"What is God doing?" I asked.

He then asked me a question that has since changed my life: "Lee, what are you now doing for the Kingdom?"

I sat back and thought for a moment. "Well, I meet with men on a regular basis. I get with them and try to become their friend, and then I try to help them in any way I can."

"Have you ever considered doing that as a ministry?" Jim asked.

"Can I do that, Jim?" I responded.

"Sure," he said. "Bloom where God has you planted."

Over the next couple of months, I sought the counsel of a friend, Roger Sowder, and our church elders at Christ Community Church in Simpsonville, SC. I also searched the Scriptures to see if this was a viable ministry. Everywhere I seemed to go only confirmed Jim's advice.

It was especially solidified when I saw Jesus constantly having one-on-one encounters throughout his ministry in the Gospels. In Matthew, I've now noted Jesus had 25 one-on-one encounters; in Mark, 24; in Luke, 26; and in John, 21. So, if my records are correct, Jesus had almost one hundred one-on-one, face-to-face encounters with individuals throughout his ministry. And those are only the ones we know about!

It is amazing to me that so many of our seminaries and Bible schools often don't teach this. Instead, they teach how to build and pastor churches and how to start small groups and Bible studies, but they teach very little—if anything— on how to build relationships with others. Yet, was this not what Jesus spent most of his time doing?

To corroborate my findings, I looked at the life of Jesus and observed three categories:

(1) Jesus in large group settings (i.e., the feeding of the five thousand)
(2) Jesus in small group settings (i.e., the disciples at the last supper)
(3) Jesus in one-on-one encounters (i.e., the woman at the well)

My conclusions were staggering as my findings substantiated the following:

- Percentage of time Jesus spent in large group settings = 15%
- Percentage of time Jesus spent in small group settings = 35%
- Percentage of time Jesus spent in one-on-one encounters = 50%

(Note: With these findings, please allow for a small margin of error in either direction.)

Now that I had this information in hand, I also noted how many of our churches have been trained to look to the pastors to do the work of evangelism. I feel that in most cases, lay people have been taught to feel incompetent as they don't know how to preach, build churches, or teach Bible studies. Therefore, they aren't confident when sharing their lives and faith with other individuals.

When I saw this error in our churches, it also dawned on me that anyone could be a friend. You don't have to go to a Bible school or seminary to develop relationships with others.

As the evidence mounted, I saw a real need. Soon, One-on-One Ministries was formed. Since that meeting with Jim, we have grown to become an international ministry. We do speaking engagements, conferences, write materials, correspond via email, and are growing in other areas even as I write.

Most importantly, we continue to befriend others on a daily basis. We just cannot get away from the fact that as Jesus came to seek and to save the lost, he often did it through the means of establishing friendships.

He has now called us to take the same gospel to others in the same way in which he modeled it for us.

I'll close with this story as I like to give examples frequently to encourage my readers as well as to show them how easy it is to engage and develop friendships for Christ.

It was a late, cold winter night. I was driving back from college. I saw two people walking. They were out in the middle of nowhere, hitchhiking and wearing little clothing. I stopped and picked them up, which is something I no longer do much of now, nor do I recommend this practice in today's society.

Dave and Brad had been hitchhiking around the country when they were recently robbed and had everything stolen, including their clothes. They hadn't eaten in a while, so I took them a truck stop and got them something to eat.

As Brad left us to find out directions to their destination, I started talking to Dave. I could tell he was hurting, so I shared my life with him and told him how Christ had changed things for me.

Instantly, I could sense he wanted to know more, so I shared how he could trust Christ also and become a Christian. Within moments, I saw the birth of a new creature in Christ take place before my very eyes.

When Brad returned to the table, I tried to share the same thing with him, but he wanted nothing of it. As we departed, I knew I might never see Dave again on this earth, but I also knew that I'd see a brother again one day in heaven!

What a joy and pleasure it is to see God work in our midst and to be a part of his harvest here on earth? All it takes is to be a friend, and anyone can do that!

Was this not what our Lord was constantly doing? Jesus went about doing good, constantly showing himself friendly. It is a known fact that our Lord was a friend to sinners.

Are we?

PRACTICAL APPLICATION

Throughout our conferences, we continue the practice of dividing into small groups of four people. At this juncture, each group is asked to turn to the book of *Mark*. Each person in each group is given four chapters in the book, which totals 16 chapters, and then they are asked to survey their assigned chapters over the next twenty minutes.

Each person's objective is to note how many one-on-one encounters Jesus is observed having. We then ask them to share their findings and come up with a total number for the whole book. We add these totals together for Mark, along with Matthew's 25, Luke's 26, and John's 27.

This gives us a good Biblical foundation and methodology for evangelism to address and substantiate for ourselves. It also allows us to take our findings back to our friends and churches to teach and also model before them.

CHAPTER THREE

A FRIENDLY LIFESTYLE

"A word aptly spoken is like apples of gold in settings of silver."
Proverbs 25:11

Have you ever met a person who was pessimistic and negative about anything and everything you say? I'm sure you have. We all have.

One pastor moved into a desolate area. Besides him, there was only one other pastor in the region. Unfortunately, the other pastor was very negative.

Over time, these two became friends, but the new pastor eventually got sick of the other's pessimistic spirit. One day, he got a great idea. He would show his negative friend something he could say nothing negative about.

He had taught his dog to walk on water. He would take his friend duck hunting and show off his dog's amazing ability. Surely, his friend could say nothing negative.

Finally, the day came, and the two went hunting. Soon, a duck was shot and landed in the water. The new pastor sent his dog to get the duck. Like a skater on ice, the dog walked beautifully across the top of the water, got the duck, brought it back, and set it at the two men's feet.

"So, my dear pastor friend, what do you think about that?" inquired the new pastor, smiling.

In reply, his friend said, "That has to be the dumbest dog I've ever seen. Why, he doesn't even know how to swim!"

When we try to reach out to others, it may often seem hard to some. Many fear saying the wrong things, so they say nothing.

When I was in junior high school, I started liking girls as most young boys do about then. The one thing that seemed to hinder me was that I didn't know what to say to them. It scared me silly.

One night, I wanted to call a girl, but I had no idea what I was going to say to her. So, I got out a piece of paper and wrote down 10 to 12 items to talk about. I thought surely this would be plenty of information for a 20-minute conversation. Boy, was I wrong. I went through that list in two minutes, and then I did not know what to do. I ended up saying, "I'd better go. Goodbye."

I truly believe fear is one of the greatest obstacles we face, if not the greatest. Knowing what to say and when to say it scares most of us to death.

So, how do we deal with our fears, and what do we say when we are starting to build relationships with others? That is our main focus of this section as we learn how easy it is to speak the proper words at the right time.

I hope you are ready for this section. This is where the rubber will meet the road as we learn to "be a friend."

As we now address this topic, it is also important for us to remember a couple things: first, this is Biblical, and it is a great model that the Lord himself used throughout his life; and second, it is imperative that we all learn to be good listeners as the Apostle James calls us all to be swift to hear and slow to speak.

DIVINE APPOINTMENTS

Have you ever considered that one-on-one encounters with other individuals have been predestined and ordained by God? As we develop a friendly disposition toward those whom God brings across our paths, it is important for us to know that these are not random acts of nature but are actually divine appointments set up and orchestrated by our King himself.

Let me ask you a few questions to start. Was it an accident or a happenstance that you born where you were?

Was it just by chance that you live where you live and work where you work? Could it just be a freak thing of nature that you are where you are in life, spending it with whomever you do?

The answers are definitely "NO!" Not if you and I believe God is totally sovereign, in control of all things, and the absolute Ruler over the affairs of mankind.

So, it is no accident, chance, or happenstance that we were born where we were, live and work where we do, or spend time around those whom we call our family and friends. Nor is it a freak thing of nature that you cross paths with those whom you do on a daily basis.

Instead, a Christian who truly believes God to be sovereign sees each and every aspect of his or her life as being divinely set by God. This includes those people we encounter in our daily lives that God has ordained for us to meet and has predestined us to befriend. Let me give a couple more examples.

"Lord," I prayed a few months ago, "Would you please bless One-on-One Ministries and cause it to grow?" A few minutes later, the phone rang. It was Charlie, the Anglican Minister I'd recently met in our city of Greenville, SC.

"Lee," he said. "I'd like to do an outreach conference at our church toward the end of October, and I'd like for you to come and be our keynote speaker."

I don't believe it was by accident that God had Charlie and I meet months earlier. I don't believe it was by accident that Charlie called me that day to ask me to speak at his conference.

What I do believe is that divine appointments are everywhere. They are happening every moment of every day.

Three months ago, I decided to take my daily walk early as I had a meeting that night. I hadn't been out the door ten minutes when an old gentleman spoke to me as he was moving his trash can to the garage from the street.

I stopped. We talked about the trash, where I lived, and our city government. I introduced myself, and Mr. Mann did likewise. I departed a few minutes later with another new relationship in the neighborhood.

"Thank you, Lord, for giving me this acquaintance with Mr. Mann," I prayed as I walked away.

I don't feel this was by chance or happenstance that we met. Do you?

Again, I was out for my evening stroll. One house down, I saw Mark. He turned off his riding lawnmower, and I knew it was time to talk. Divine appointments can often change our schedules. "Man plans his ways but God directs his paths" (Proverbs 16:9).

Mark and I had become friends. He told me he was moving to Barbados for three years on a new job assignment. Interesting, isn't it? I now know somebody in Barbados. Who knows what God has in store with his divine appointments?

I soon left Mark. The time was getting late. Forget about being home before dark. As a matter of fact, the sun would be well over the ridge by the time I arrived home.

I'd been asking God recently how he danced over me (Zephaniah 3:17). As I was finishing my walk, He surprised me. A little star was twinkling in the distance and dancing in the great expanse of space. My father had given me an appointment with Mark so I could have a later appointment with Him. He had answered my prayer. He just wanted to show me how much He loved me.

As God brings these divine appointments into our lives, we need to respond with hearts of love and concern. The only time Jesus ever spoke directly about his heart in the New Testament, he told us that it was a kind and gentle one (Matthew 11:29-31).

Most people respond to acts of kindness. I have found that one of the best ways to show a life of concern and care comes by asking people questions about themselves.

Did you know that Jesus asked a total of 237 questions during his ministry on earth? Did you also know that, in Jesus' day, it was not always about who could give the best answer, but often it was about who could frame the best question.

Why was that?

If a person could pose the proper question, the forthcoming answer would usually solve the problem. For instance, the disciples wanted to know if it was proper to pay taxes to Rome. Jesus simply asked a question concerning a coin: "Whose image is on it?" (Luke 20:24)

The question led to the answer.

Another instance had the disciples wanting to know of Jesus' true identity. Our Lord asked, "Who do men say I am?" If you remember the situation, Peter answered, "Thou art the Son of God." Again, the question moved the conversation to the correct answer (Matthew 16:16).

In the same manner, questions do the same for us today. They lead the conversation and often move it along for the proper responses.

Several years ago, in my first pastorate, I worked part-time as a sports reporter for two small weekly newspapers. I realized quickly that those I interviewed cared nothing about me, who I was, or where I was going. What they cared about most was sharing what they deemed important. It was then up to me to ask the proper questions in order to get the right answers.

This was also something I learned as child from my mother. She used to tell me that people love to talk about themselves.

As an added note, I've also heard if you were to take a group picture, and you were included in it, who would be the first person you would look for? Why, yourself, of course!

Whether we want to admit it, we are sinful and selfish creatures. Asking others about themselves often gets to the heart of who they truly are and allows us to shed the loving light of Christ on their hearts.

So, how did I do this in the newspaper business?

I simply began doing something all reporters do. It's called the "5Ws." Who? What? When? Why? Where?

For example, "Coach, WHO are you starting in tomorrow's game?"

"Coach, WHAT do you think your chances are of beating the number one team in the state?"

"Coach, WHEN do you think you will play your second string?"

"Coach, WHY do you think your best teams always seem to be stronger defensively?"

"Coach, WHERE do you think you get the best performance from your players?"

Now, all of this might sound trite to some, but you would be amazed at all the information I can gather by asking these five questions: who, what, when, why, and where. I am not saying you have to ask them in this order, nor do you have to ask them all.

I'm simply saying that you should ask people questions using any or all of the 5Ws, and you will be amazed at the responses you will receive.

Now, let's take this into one of our everyday encounters. You are sitting in your company's break room, and a new employee is in there with you. He sits a few tables away. You get up and go over to meet him.

"Hi," you say as you extend your hand. "My name is Lee. WHAT is your name?

"Bill," he responds.

"Well, Bill, it's nice to meet you. WHAT department are you working in?"

"I'm in manufacturing, going through the training program right now."

"I see, Bill. Well, WHEN did you start in that department?"

"About two weeks ago, but I used to work in sales."

"Oh really? WHY did you leave sales, Bill?"

"It really didn't seem to be the best place for me. I'm more of a hands-on guy than a salesman."

"So, WHERE do you think they will finally place you in manufacturing once you've been trained?"

Do you see how these questions led the conversation and at the same time showed an interest in Bill and allowed him talk to me about himself? With those few short questions, I learned his name, in what department he was working, why he was working there, how long he had been there, his previous background with the company, what type of work he liked, etc.

The point is that I showed an interest him, and he won't forget it. I also constantly used his name, making him feel special.

These things, too, opened the door for Bill to know me. They provided further opportunities to speak to him again as I am now someone he now knows as an associate and acquaintance.

Also, it is important to make sure you are showing genuine love and concern for those whom you come in contact. Charles Stanley once said that the word, L-O-V-E, needs to be changed in our society to another four-letter word: C-A-R-E. There also is an old saying that says, "Don't tell me how much you love me until you first show me how much you care." Both Stanley and this old saying hold a lot of truth. People need to know we are honestly concerned about them and that we care. It's amazing how things unfold if we just show a genuine interest.

Now, let me tell you of a true-life story that actually happened to me one early morning in February. I was on my way to the YMCA for a workout, and I prayed that God would let me meet someone that I might be able to eventually befriend to Christ.

I entered the sauna around six o'clock to limber up before my workout. A gentleman sat across from me. It was just he and me, all alone.

"Hi," I said. "My name is Lee. WHAT is your name?"

"My name is Dave," he said.

"Dave, WHAT are you doing in here so early? I don't believe I've seen you before. Are you getting ready to go work out?

"No. I just finished," he replied, "I'm heading to work soon."

"So, WHERE do you work, Dave?"

"I work up the street at that company on the corner."

"WHAT is it you do?"

"I'm an engineer."

I then asked Dave what he did as an engineer, and he explained the ins and outs of his job. When he finished, I asked him how secure things were at work as I had been hearing that a lot of engineers were losing their jobs in the area. He assured me his job was safe.

By then, the sauna was almost more than I could bear. I told him I would look forward to seeing him again and wished him well. Then, two days later, I ran into Dave again, and he told me he lost his job shortly after our talk that morning.

He could not believe how we had just talked on the matter, and then that day, he was let go. Shortly after that, we began lifting weights together and soon became friends.

One day, Dave talked with me about my faith and told me he thought Christianity was nothing more than a myth. I challenged him to read the *Gospel of John* in the Bible.

Months passed as we continued to talk and deepen our friendship. Then, one day, Dave shared that he had become a believer like me. How my heart did rejoice!

Today, Dave and I stay in regular contact even though he lives miles away. I count him as a very dear friend. We often reflect on that time years ago in the sauna.

Recently, Dave wrote and said, "I can't put my finger on it or describe it in words, but you are truly a unique and fascinating man. I pray for you often. By God's grace, you came into my life and 'showed me the light.'"

Yes, God's appointments are real. He sets them up and orchestrates them each and every day of our lives.

I truly believe he has a divine appointment for you to-day. He may even have more than one.

As you encounter your next divine appointment, try asking a few questions. You'll be amazed at the responses you'll get. Who knows where it might lead. Maybe even to a sauna.

GREATEST OBSTACLE: FEAR

"Okay, Lee, you've given me a solid Biblical foundation to help develop a friendly lifestyle. You've also equipped me by encouraging me to be a good listener and one who shows a genuine interest in others as I ask them about themselves.

"So, I do feel somewhat prepared, but there is still one major hurdle I have yet to conquer, and that is the fear of putting this into action. I've got to admit that taking the first step is something that scares me to death.

"How then am I to deal with this overwhelming fear that seems to possess me?"

Let me begin by saying something first and then ex-pounding upon it. Developing a friendly lifestyle means learning above all things that we have to take to our fears to God.

The Bible says in 1 Peter 5:8, "Casting all your cares upon him for he cares for you." The Scripture does not *suggest* we do this; rather, it literally *commands* us to do it. God forbids us to do anything otherwise and actually prohibits us from not giving our fears to him.

It is an amazing fact that God tells us in the Bible 365 times not to fear. Imagine that! God has given us what I call a "do not fear vitamin" for each day of the year. Why do you think that is?

To best answer that question, let's go back to the beginning of time as we know it. Shortly after Adam and Eve were created, they sinned and ate of the Tree of the Knowledge of Good and Evil.

Later, God comes looking for them in the cool of the day and calls out to man, "Adam where are you?" Adam comes forth and says, "I was afraid... and I hid myself," (Genesis 3:10).

Isn't it interesting that the first emotion we see from Adam after his sin in the garden is fear? It is my sincere belief that fear is at the core of all of our sinful hearts. Fear is a great consequence that sin has dealt to the whole human race. We all struggle with fear and have to deal with it everyday in one form or another.

Now, let's move to fear's solution and the way to deal with it.

Jesus himself has called us to take up our cross daily and follow him. Why do you think he commanded us to do this?

At the cross, he dealt with our fears and put them to death. He bore our sins upon himself on the cross in order to set us free from the pain of sin and death.

So, what I am saying is Jesus literally took my sins and everything that is associated with them to the cross, including my fears. At that point, the Bible teaches, he put them to death and destroyed them.

We often try to hold on to our fears that are no more. God therefore says, "Let go. Give them to me. I've already dealt with them. They no longer belong to you. I paid for them with my Son's blood. I bought them and you have no right or ownership to them. Let go!"

But you say, "I don't feel like they are gone."

And I understand that! But God says our sins are gone. And his words are true whether we feel like it or not.

For instance, suppose you buy a house and are given a valid contract on the house. Then, two days later, someone comes to your door and tells you to get out of the house and that you don't own it. The person gives you several good reasons why your ownership is not good and then demands that you leave.

At first, you start to believe the person has a good point. Why, you even start to feel very uncomfortable about the situation. Then, you begin to think about your legally binding contract and what it says. You go and get it. You then read it over again and see that they are wrong, according to the contract.

You call your lawyer who recites word-for-word what is stated on your legal document. He tells you that you can count on what it says no matter what the other party tells you or how you might be feeling.

He then tells you to relax and let go of your feelings because you have nothing to fear. The contract is valid because your funds secured your ownership of the house. Therefore, there is no reason to fear. Relax.

I believe you get the point, or at least, I hope you do. God says he paid the price to set us free from the pain of sin and death, and fear is definitely associated with these. He paid the price in order to set us free. The Bible says, "He who the Son sets us free is free indeed" (John 8:36). There is no doubt about it. What has been stated by the contract of God's Word can be counted upon legally no matter what anyone may say or how you or I may feel.

"So, what happens when I feel fearful?"

Do exactly what God says, and run to the cross. Remind yourself of the truth and begin walking in it whether you feel like it or not. Do it with the firm confidence in what God has said is true. Stand on it with all your strength.

The Bible tells us in 2 Timothy 1:7 to be bold in our faith. Paul reminds Timothy that he is not to live a cowardly or timid lifestyle. Instead, he is to live a life of power and boldness that stands on the truth of what God has said is true.

We are called to do the same. When these fears come, run to the cross and be reminded of the truth. Then, stand on it. Do all that is necessary to live in the reality of what God says is true, no matter what is telling you otherwise. God commands us to do this each and every day. As we do, we will find that our fears in these areas will start to subside as we begin to take that step of faith, trusting what God says.

This is very important. What I am speaking about is non-negotiable. It is the way of the Christian and a huge answer in learning to "Be a Friend: One-on-One."

PRACTICAL APPLICATION

A good practice in which we now engage at our confer-ences is to have our groups of four begin working on the 5Ws. We have one person ask another person questions for a period of five minutes while the other two in the group observe.

Once the first pair completes their allotted five-minute time period, it then moves to the next pair until each person has had a chance to ask questions and to give answers. The time cycle should take no longer than 20 minutes.

We have found that people are amazed at how easy this is to do and how much they learn about the others during this time. It also gives them a practice field of preparation in lieu of befriending others in real life.

CHAPTER FOUR

A PRAYING LIFESTYLE

"Praying with all prayer and supplication in the spirit
And watching unto with all perseverance and supplication for all
saints; And for me, that utterance may be given unto me,
That I may open my mouth boldly, to make known the
mystery of the gospel, For which I am an ambassador in bonds;
that therein I may speak boldly, As I ought to speak."
Ephesians 6:18-20

There is an old myth, which is fictional, that still packs a lot of power. This story can be found in Joe Alrich's book, *Lifestyle Evangelism*. It has to do with Jesus' arrival to heaven shortly after the resurrection. The angels of heaven gather around the throne to welcome the Lord home. A short while later, one of the angel's asks, "Lord, you left eleven disciples on earth to carry forth your message to the whole world. Now, let's suppose these eleven fail. What is your Plan B?"

Jesus looked at him confidently and said, "There is no Plan B."

Jesus continues today, working his one and only plan, and he has called you and I to be a part of it. What a thrilling honor to be included in reaching the world with the gospel!

In the last three chapters, we have looked at various aspects of befriending others as we carry out his plan. Such things involve recognizing that this is Biblical, God gives divine appointments, he calls us to show loving concern and care while being good listeners and askers of questions, and that we must refer our fears to God's Word and the work of Christ on the cross.

As we move into our last and final chapter of this book, I want to convey the importance of prayer. Like each chapter before, I hope to change our perspective on this subject.

Dr. Jerry Falwell once said, "Nothing of eternal value is ever accomplished apart from prayer." Have you ever considered that prayer is two-fold? I will begin by explaining what I mean in a story involving two women.

Jeanette knocked on the door of her friend's home.

"Come in," Margaret said.

As Jeanette came through the door, she noticed Margaret was on her knees praying.

"Margaret," Jeanette inquired, "Why are you praying?"

"Jeanette, I am praying about that sleazy old beer tavern across the street. It's a sinful and wicked place. I'm praying God will burn that thing down. I've been praying that prayer for thirty-eight years."

"Well, could I then pray with you about it?" Jeanette inquired.

"Sure," Margaret replied.

So, for the next ten minutes, Margaret and Jeanette prayed for God to burn the old tavern down. That very same night, it burned to the ground.

When Jeanette arrived at Margaret's the next day, she said to her, "I can't believe it Jeanette! I've been praying for 38 years for that old tavern to burn down, and you prayed with me one time, and it burned to the ground last night. Now, how is that?"

"Very simply," Jeanette replied. "You see, Margaret, I put feet to my prayers!"

Although this is a cute little joke, and I do not encourage what Jeanette did by any means, there still is a lot of truth to it. Prayer is two-fold: (1) it requires petitioning the throne of grace; and (2) it requires putting our faith and prayers into action.

PETITIONING GOD

A prayerful lifestyle first involves petitioning God on behalf of others. If we aren't praying for them, who is?

My Greek professor in seminary, Dr. Ron Sower, first made this challenge to me. I'll never forget that day when he came into our class and said to the small group of 14 young men, "Christians are the only people on the face of God's earth who can pray for other people. And gentlemen, if you are not praying for others, then who is?"

That was one of those "God moments" for sure. It made a great impact on me and continues to do so to this day because of its relevance. As believers, we are to pray for others constantly in order to fulfill God's plan and our role in his work.

"But," you say, "I can't find time to always go and find a room alone to kneel and pray."

Who says you always have to pray in a back room on your knees? Some of the greatest prayer warriors I know did not necessarily always pray on their knees. Some of the greatest men and women have prayed while walking, driving, riding on a bicycle, sitting in a Lazy Boy chair, or sitting on their back porch at a picnic table. The place and stance are not the issues.

The questions are, "Are you praying or not?" and "If you are not, then who is?" You and I cannot assume that someone else is praying. God has called all of us to pray. Therefore, I cannot help but echo the words of Dr. Sower again: "Christians are the only people on the face of God's earth who can pray for other people. And gentlemen, if you are not praying for others, then who is?"

PARTICIPATING IN GOD'S WORK

A prayerful lifestyle not only involves petitioning God on behalf of others, but also participating in God's work. In the same manner, if we are not putting our faith into action, then who can we count on to do it?

One of my dearest friends is a fellow named Rob Buck. I've known Rob since I was in diapers. We grew up together and have kept a close friendship over these many years.

As I was passing through Columbia, SC late one evening, Rob asked me to give him a call. He said he'd like to meet me for coffee somewhere to share something very important.

Because it was so late, we met at a small, off-the-road diner and ordered our food. Once we finished, I asked Rob if he could go ahead and share his important news. It was then that he told me one of the craziest yet most profound things I have ever heard.

"Lee," he said, "I've been asking God to help me to understand life, and recently, he showed me."

"Really?" I said. "And what exactly did he show you, Rob?"

"Well," he replied, "God showed me life is like as a set of railroad tracks."

"A set of railroad tracks?" I must admit I was a little mystified by his statement.

"That's right," Rob responded excitedly, "Railroad tracks. He showed me that my railroad tracks of life have hills and valleys, twists and turns."

"Okay," I said. "I can see that."

"But that's not all God showed me. Lee, he showed me that my railroad tracks are constantly intersecting with other people's railroad tracks."

"Yes, I can see that, too." It was starting to make some sense.

"But here's the exciting part." Rob's eyes were now wide open with exhilaration. "Lee, I asked God to show me why he lets my railroad tracks intersect with other people's railroad tracks, and he showed me!"

It was then I sat up in my seat. "Rob, you've got my full attention."

Rob smiled and said, "It's for his glory."

Well, I knew that and for a moment, my bubble was burst. But then Rob said, "But I wanted to know specifically why it was for his glory, and he showed me."

Again, he had my full attention.

"Watch this, Lee." At that moment, our waitress came back to the table. Her name was Cathy.

"Cathy," Rob said, "We certainly did appreciate your service, but before we go, I'd like to ask you a question?"

"Sure," she replied.

"My friend, Lee, and I are old friends, and he was just passing through town and stopped to visit with me for a little while. Both of us are also Christians, and we like to pray for people. Cathy, I'd like to ask you if there is anything Lee and I could pray for you about."

Almost instantly, tears welled up in Cathy's eyes as she responded, "Yes, you can. My husband and I just lost our only boy in childbirth, and it has about killed us. Yes, could you please pray for my husband and me?"

Over the next minute or two, I watched Rob show loving concern and care for Cathy as he asked her a few questions and showed interest in her problem. He then promised her that when we got out in the parking lot, we would pray for her and her husband, the very thing we did.

I left there spellbound at the story of the railroad tracks and the example I witnessed before my eyes. Fifty miles later, I stopped for some gas off the interstate.

A woman named Shawna was alone, running the convenience store. For some strange reason, I asked her if it got lonely out there being this late as it was almost 1:30 in the morning.

"No," she answered. "You see, several years ago, my only son was killed by some friends. It rocked my world. For over two years, I could not leave my house. Recently, the doctor told me I had to get out and do something. So, yes, it's quiet. But I truly think it's what I need at this point in my life."

As I rode away, I thought of Rob's story of the railroad tracks. It was not any accident Cathy was our waitress and Shawna was working the late shift when I stopped for gas.

You see, God's glory ushered forth a reason for allowing our railroad tracks to cross with theirs. And he does the same for you and me every day of our lives.

I have used Rob's story and example countless times in my own life. If God seems to be giving me a connection with a waiter or waitress, I also thank them for their service. I then share with them that I am a Christian and ask if there is anything I could be praying for them about. I have never received a negative comment, but I usually get a positive response.

It's truly been an amazing adventure. I can't wait to see whose railroad tracks I cross tomorrow. How about you?

Here's another story. My mother started attending an Anglican church in town. Later, she introduced me to Pastor Charlie, and we quickly became friends.

One evening, we met for supper. Immediately, we built a relationship with our waitress, Cindy. At the end of the meal, I asked her if there was anything Charlie and I could be praying for her about.

Cindy then shared that she had cancer, and her husband was without a job. We told her we would definitely pray for them both, thanked her, and left.

Three months later, Charlie and I were eating there again, and Cindy was waiting on us. She looked different, but not being sure it was her, I asked, "Are you that young lady that served us three months ago, the one we told we would pray for?"

"Yes," she answered with a smile, and I could see immediately that she had some good news for us. "I'm so glad to see you two. So much has happened since I last talked to you guys that day. I no longer have my cancer, my husband has a job, and we are now going to church."

Not only was it exciting for Cindy, but also it was great news for Charlie and me. Two months later, Charlie had me do my first One-on-One Ministry Conference in his church.

There, he shared the story of Cindy, and I also shared Rob's story of the railroad tracks. I told of Cathy, Shawna, and many more. What was so exciting is that these stories don't have to be just Charlie's, Rob's, or mine. They can be yours, too!

In closing, I'd like to cover one final thing concerning a prayerful lifestyle. It, too, involves actualizing or appropriating what God can do in each of our lives.

Rob Buck and I have had many usual encounters together over the years. One involved a penny Rob found in a parking lot one day. Did you know that if you take a penny and double it 28 times, you would have over a million dollars?

"Preposterous!" you might say.

No, do the math. You'll be shocked.

Anyway, to continue my story, Rob and I decided we would give this penny a shot on the road of life and see if we could take it to a million dollars. We almost did it until we invested our money in a venture that went south, and we lost all but $37. Nonetheless, we had the time of our lives buying and selling the craziest things you can imagine and doing it together.

But more than anything, Rob and I saw the possibility of this really happening. Since then, I have come to see the same reality in the power of one person reaching another person, those two reaching two, etc.

Now, bear with me for a moment. Did you know that you—numero uno, number one; yes, you—have the power and capability to reach the world for Jesus Christ in a span of thirty to forty years?

That's right! You have the opportunity to reach the entire world just by befriending one person a year for Christ!

If you are a pastor, let's say with 32 members, there is no reason why you can't ask each person to make one new friend over the next year. If you and your congregation will commit to doing this each year, it is possible for your congregation to reach the entire world for Jesus Christ in twenty-seven years.

"Preposterous!" you say again.

Well, let's look at the math in just a moment. As we do, think about this: who would have thought that those eleven disciples would have ever made the impact they did.

Think and pray about it. D.L. Moody, a famous evangelist from the 1800s, once said, "The world has yet to see what God can do with a man fully consecrated to him. By God's help, I aim to be that man. "

Do we believe our God can do great and mighty things in our midst? Do we pray, realizing we are actually called to reach our world with the gospel of Jesus Christ?

I believe we can—one at a time, one-on-one—reach our world by simply learning to "Be a Friend." Do you believe it? Judge for yourself.

Beginning with you and a congregation of 32 people...

Years	Kingdom Growth
1	32
2	64
3	128
4	256
5	512
6	1,024
7	2,028
8	4,056
9	8,112
10	16,224
11	32,448
12	64,896
13	129,792
14	259,584

15	519,168
16	1,028,336
17	2,056,672
18	4,113,344
19	8,226,688
20	16,453,376
21	32,906,742
22	65,813,484
23	131,626,968
24	263,253,936
25	526,507,872
26	1,053,015,744
27	2,106,031,488
28	4,212,062,576

PRACTICAL APPLICATION

As we close our conferences, I have our groups of four meet one last time to pray together. If someone does not feel comfortable doing this, they just pass on their turn.

What is beautiful are relationships that have been formed during these times. People leave having made new friends. It is always my hope that some of these relationships will continue to grow.

As for me, it certainly has been a privilege to share this material with you. I hope you will implement what you have learned and begin developing friendships with those you encounter, that is, those whom God lets cross your railroad tracks of life.

Could I ask you one thing further? As you know, I am a Christian, and it has been a joy to share what the Lord has laid on my heart. And as a Christian and sharer of this good news, I like to pray for people. Therefore, if there is ever anything I could be praying for you about, please do not hesitate to let me know. I would count it a joy to bring your petition before our Father's heavenly throne.

Because we are now in the conversation and spirit of prayer, I would like to beckon our King with a closing prayer and benediction.

CLOSING PRAYER & BENEDICTION

Father, I thank you for this book and the people who have read its contents. We cannot help but see that befriending others was a vital part of the ministry and work of our Lord Jesus.

For many of us, we have often passed people in our lives that were hurting and seeking a friend. We often overlooked them when you sent them to us, and for this, we are truly sorry.

Take our lives now and use these encounters for your honor and glory. Help us to see others with your eyes. Help us to be a friend to them as Jesus was a friend to sinners.

We thank you for the light you have shown us in this study. Now, may we be faithful stewards of what you have entrusted to our care. For we pray these things in the precious name of our Lord and Savior, Jesus Christ. Amen.

"And now unto the King eternal, immortal, invisible,
The only wise God,
Be honor and glory, both now and forever. Amen."
(1 Timothy 1:17)

APPENDIX

Shortly after the conception of One-on-One Ministries, I formed an advisory board of twelve men and gave it the name, "The Table of Twelve." To this group, I began sending out a monthly newsletter concerning this ministry and its development. Often, I would ask questions, give updates, and share stories of one-on-one encounters with others.

After the first year of operation, I saw a need to have others join with us. It was not long before our mailing list grew to over one hundred subscribers.

What follows are several of those letters. I felt it would be beneficial to include these for your reading as they relate well to the material in this book and can be used as a guide to reach out and befriend others for the glory of our Lord and King. (Throughout the book, as with these letters, some names and situations have been slightly altered in order to be sensitive to other's privacy.)

TO: My Dear Friends Whom I Call: *"THE TABLE OF TWELVE"* (August 2006)

Greetings! I hope this letter finds you all doing well and in good health.

Since my last letter, God has graciously done a lot in the development of *"One-on-One Ministries."* The state of

South Carolina has approved this ministry, I now have a federal ID number and a bank account, and we are in the midst of forming our board in order to move a head with the 501(c)(3) non-profit corporation status.

In the meantime and more importantly, I continue to meet with men whenever I can.

Just recently, the Greenville newspaper reported that a survey had been taken, which concluded that the average man today goes to his grave without having one real close friend. To me, that is horrifying! It also confirms the need for more ministries like this and for us to reach out to others in love. If for nothing more, we just need to give people a friend. Is this not what the Lord was constantly doing? Jesus was known as a "friend to sinners," which is what we all are.

I also mentioned in my last letter that I was going to write a question for you each month as it concerned relationships so that I could get your input. After some counsel, I have decided to tweak this somewhat by writing periodically to ask your advice. This might mean more than once a month or possibly once a quarter, but it will be whenever I deem an issue needs your counsel.

So, here is my question today, and I will preface it some.

It is always my intent to communicate that I care for the other gentleman with whom I am meeting. My desire is to get beyond general conversation and to the things that really matter in their lives. Sometimes, this takes much prayer, time, and patience. My question is,

"How do you really show or demonstrate a caring heart toward another man you are befriending? What is it you do and/or say that you have found helpful in reaching out to the one sitting before you?"

I do appreciate so much any thoughts you can give. I also want you to know that I appreciate each one of you as you are each very special to me. And now may God also bless you, too, in your friendships with others.

Sincerely,
Your Friend, Lee

P.S. You are in my prayers.

Question: "How do you really show or demonstrate a caring heart toward another man you are befriending? What is it you do and/or say that you have found helpful in reaching out to the one sitting before you?"

Answer: "Take advantage of opportunities to serve. Listen to what he has to say. Don't judge, but love unconditionally. Hold him up before the throne in prayer. Be available as often as possible to assist. Lift him up through encouragement and counsel. Empathize with his plight. Point him to the cross of mercy and grace. Remind him that it is all about Jesus. Challenge, motivate, and disciple him. Instill self-respect and discipline to stay on the narrow path. Let him know it is okay to cry." (TL)

Answer: I think that asking questions and really exhibiting active listening shows love. Listening without condemning or lecturing in return. Men will be drawn to that. Also, seeing yourself as the chief sinner. Others are attracted to those who struggle—not to those who appear to have it all together. Being willing to struggle together—perhaps in different areas—but struggling." (JP)

Answer: "Two things come to my mind… the first is invest time. The strongest relationships I have are with people that I spend time with. You can meet someone's needs by giving money or letting them borrow something, but it does not yield the same relational value as investing face-to-face time together. And the friendships I developed by spending lots of time together are the ones that have stood the test of time and distance. The second thing I think of is being equally as vulnerable. I cannot expect a friend to open up to me if I'm not willing to open up to them with the same level of transparency… and not necessarily being MORE transparent because that can scare off or close doors as well, but being equally trusting with each other. (MM)

Answer: "I think to care for a man, we need to be aware of his condition, physically, mentally, emotionally, and of course, spiritually. This comes by genuine conversation and questions. Determining where they struggle, what makes their hearts come alive, and the details of their lives conveys that you care. Everyone has a story; make it your goal to learn theirs. As time goes on, trust will be developed, and they will begin to let down their guard, hopeful-ly. Sometimes, this is very difficult with men. Make it your goal to help them progress to the next step in their spiritual lives but never at the expense of their other needs." (RB)

Answer: "How easy it is to give lip service but not go any further. For example, it's easy to say "hello" at church or nod your head, but no one asks the new couple to lunch after the service. Most skid-addle to the restaurant or home. Going the extra step to involve yourself in someone else's life demonstrates interest and isn't that what is necessary to minister? Another characteristic of the one who wants to make a difference is to be vulnerable. If we are willing to share our inner struggles, then the other person's facade can be lowered. Careful: it must be framed in trust!" (TC)

Answer: "I just have found, in 2006, people see right through anything that isn't genuine. (I am sure it has been much longer, but I just hadn't noticed it.) Being a genuine, loving, gracious person with whomever always is the bottom line. Everything, and I mean everything, springs forth from that." (JC)

Answer: "1) Contact him - by phone, visit, or emails. 2) Communicate with him - look him in the eye and have genuine heartfelt conversation. 3) Challenge him - let him know that you have his best interest in mind by challeng-ing him to take whatever you might perceive to be the next step in his personal spiritual journey." (BB)

Answer: "I try to give him all the "floor time" he seems to want and listen to what he has to say. Then, I indicate that he has valid points in his conversation and go from there; but, at some point in our conversation, I try to bring up the Lord in some way. I don't preach to him or judge him, but I offer the Lord's take on whatever issue he may be facing. I guess, to answer your question, I listen more than talk. Then, we'll see where, if anywhere, the relationship goes." (KJ)

Answer: "I just try to be supportive in any way I can. It could be monetary, philosophical, spiritual, or just plain casual listening. Really, it is a function of what their needs are at that specific time. If there is a way I can help, I would most certainly do it." (DM)

TO: My Dear Friends Whom I Call: "THE TABLE OF TWELVE" (September 2006)

Greetings! I hope this letter finds you all doing well and in good health. Please do let me know how things are going and if there is anything I can be praying about for you.

As for us, we are in the midst of moving to Greenville, SC so our daughter, Hannah, might be able to attend a special school in the area. I am also finally coming to the realization that I am definitely getting older as my mind is now starting to face the fact of what my body has been voicing for years: "Lee, you're not the young buck you once were." Nancy and I see our moving days are about over as we're reaching the "50" barrier.

I did so much appreciate the many responses I got from my question I posed last month. As part of this correspondence, I have discreetly taken excerpts from your letters. In order to keep each person's identity private, I have placed your initials beside each one below in the event anyone might like to comment on another's response.

As for One-on-One Ministries, we have hit a momentary wall. Our move to Greenville has taken a lot of time, and then there is my job situation. I'm doing several part-time things right now to help make ends meet, but I need to have something more permanent as Nancy is no longer teaching. I mention this in order to ask you to keep us in your prayers.

I continue to meet with men when I can as God graciously puts people and opportunities before me. I am also constantly bombarded with the reality that "men need men" more than they know. A two-year-old blockbuster study labeled, "Social Isolation in America," recently said the following:

> A face-to-face study of 1,467 adults turned up some disheartening news. One-fourth of all Americans report that they have no one to talk about 'important matters.' Another quarter reports they are just one person away from nobody. But this was the most startling fact. The study is a replica of one done 20 years ago. In only two decades, from 1985 to 2004, the number of people who have no one to talk to has doubled.

This is mind-blowing, is it not, my brothers? Isolation and loneliness are quickly becoming an epidemic in our culture. Therefore, I encourage you to ask God to help you reach out to someone in need over next couple of months and become their friend.

Jesus said, "I tell you the truth, whatever you did for one of the least of these brothers of mine, you did for me" (Matthew 10:40). My prayers are with you as you go,

Your Friend,
Lee Moseley

P.S. Please do let me know your thoughts on the responses listed below.

TO: My Dear Friends Whom I Call: "THE TABLE OF TWELVE" (October 2006)

Fall is upon us, and the crisp cool morning air says winter is around the corner as the leaves in South Carolina are now starting to spin their colors. With this yearly occurrence, I cannot help but think of the changes in our lives as new horizons confront us daily.

This past month has been exciting. Recently, I had the pleasure of running into an old friend I had not seen for almost 30 years. We sat in a restaurant and talked for almost two hours. The greatest part of the story came when I heard him share of his walk with Christ. Years ago, I remember praying that he would come to know the Lord and before my very eyes, I witnessed God's grace in my friend after all these years. How exciting!

I have also taken on a part-time job shuttling folks from one parking lot to another. These are some very bright men and women from all over the world. They have come to work at a very special automotive research center that has been developed in conjunction with BMW, Clemson University, the State of SC, and many other huge corporations.

Often, in my trips from one parking lot to another, God gives me opportunity to share my life and faith. From the conversations, the Lord has begun to develop relationships with some whom I feel are fast becoming my friends. I have also seen God at work as He has given me some other relations with fellow believers scattered throughout the groups.

How exciting it is to be a part in God's harvest fields. How exciting it is to meet new people who let me into their lives and are curious to discuss things of vital importance. When it is all said and done, what it comes down to is being a friend, which is what our Lord himself modeled for us.

That leads me to the next question I would like to pose to you, my brothers on the Table of Twelve. Plain and simply, *"What is a friend? I mean, what does a friend look like when you think about one?"*

I think this is an important question if we are to be a friend to others. Jesus was known as a friend to sinners. So, what does that mean when it is fleshed out in our lives? I leave that question with you to ponder, and I look forward to your response.

Keep us in your prayers as I am now talking with a church about the possibility of filling their Sr. Pastor position in Gaffney, SC. Also, pray for our family as things have been very tough these past two years, both emotionally and financially. My prayers are lifted up for each of you daily. Please do stay in touch with me, one-on-one.

Your Friend,
Lee

TO: My Dear Friends Whom I Call: "THE TABLE OF TWELVE" (November 2006)

It's Halloween! What an open door God gave me this morning as I had the opportunity to cast some gospel seed. On my shuttle van, I carry many businessmen and women to their job sites. In the process, I often have opportunities to discuss parts of my faith. Today was such a moment as I shared about the history of Halloween and the Reformation.

On occasions, God has opened many doors with this new part-time job. We recently had Don, a Vietnamese gentleman, over to our house to eat and have family devotions. Kon, a German engineer, will be coming over tomorrow night for the same.

Peter and a female co-worker of his, Helen, from Connecticut called Sunday morning, asking if they could accompany Nancy and I to church to hear me preach. It is amazing how hungry people are for the gospel. Are not "the fields white unto harvest?"

I'm attaching some great responses below which some of you sent back in reply to my questions: *"What is a friend? What does a friend look like when you think about it?"* I believe you will find the answers I received to be encouraging as some of you have stated.

This month, I would like to leave our Table of Twelve with the following: *"Why is it so important to address a person by name? Why is it that one's name is so significant?"* When Jesus addressed others, he often called them by name. And if Jesus deemed this of much value, should we not also?

When I first started driving the shuttle van, I had a desire to try and learn all 180 passengers by name. (I would say I'm at about 75% now.) Nonetheless, I have seen God move in the lives of many of my new friends when I call them by their names. It seems to make an immediate caring, relational connection as I am seeing God open many hearts.

Mike recently asked me to pray for his marriage.

Denny asked for prayer for his sick father.

Kary shared of his divorce.

Ron and I have ongoing, friendly discussions about his involvement with the Jehovah Witnesses.

Kevin, an atheist, talks with me often about his philosophical views and has even asked me to go to supper with him this week.

I guess you can see how God has been using this experience in my life to share the gospel. I'm excited about it as you can see. So, I pose these questions to you this month, my dearly beloved brothers of the Table of Twelve: *"Why is it so important to address a person by name? And why is it that one's name is so significant?"*

I leave you with these things to consider. I pray for you each daily by name. Each one of you has played a very special part in my life as we have developed relationships over time, one-on-one with one another. May God Bless you, my friends. Pray for us here.

Your Friend,
Lee

Question: *What is a friend? What does a friend look like when you think about it?*

Answer: "A FRIEND is someone who has your best interest in mind – and sometimes, we really don't even know what our best interest is. Always, though, our best interest is to know and do the will of God – whether we realize it or not." (BB)

Answer: "When I think of 'what is a friend,' I obviously think of someone that is more than just an acquaintance. I think of someone who is a kindred spirit. My true friends help guide me in the truth, even if it hurts. When I think about what a friendship looks like, I am reminded of David and Jonathan whose souls were 'knit together.' Deep friendships are up front with one another, asking loving questions, never putting the other down behind their backs. I heard it said once that a true friendship 'always seeks the other person's highest good.' Relationships like this will endure the tests of time, distance, and any trial. Real friendships don't just happen; they are hard work... keeping accountability to become all God wants us to be." (M/M)

Answer: "A friend is a constant companion who cares to confront, consistently encourages, unconditionally loves, and who gives without thought of reciprocation." (TL)

Answer: "To me, a friend is someone who you can trust to hold a confidence, a person who really does care about you, someone you enjoy being with and talking to, someone you can be truly honest with, will care enough not to give you a pat answer, someone who is on the same journey as you and can relate, and someone you can have fun with." (RB)

TO: My Dear Friends Whom I Call: "THE TABLE OF TWELVE" (December 2006)

Last month, I asked, *"Why is it so important to address a person by name? Why is it that one's name is so significant?"* I received some good comments and am placing them at the end of this letter for your perusal in hopes that these might benefit you and your ministry with others, one-on-one.

I pray for you each and every day and am thankful for your friendship. I truly hope all is going well with you and your families. I do desire to follow your lives more closely so I can better pray for you in the future and regarding the things you are encountering in your daily lives. So, please do keep me informed.

Prayer is also the subject of my letter today. I am finding myself in prayer more now than ever before. Spending time with the Lord in prayer and in the reading of His Word before my family arises in the morning has now become a daily practice. It is also something I find I need and have come to enjoy.

Not only that, but before my very eyes, I have come to see my prayers answered daily in ways the world might tag as unusual, but as God's child, one would see as coming from the Father's love. What a joy it is to experience His work and grace in my life.

Prayer is a strange thing; is it not? Yet, it is the very thing God calls us to do. It has power before the throne of heaven and moves God's work upon this earth. I have pondered prayer much during this past month and have come to the conclusion that it is God's pleasing instrument that he has made available for His children to access Him. Perhaps we could see it, in a sense, like the cell phones I purchased my teenagers in order for them to get in touch with me.

For whatever reason, God delights in the prayers of His saints. He actually delights in hearing from his children and bringing their petitions before Him. Often, we miss out because we do not pray. I place this thought before you today, my friends on "The Table of Twelve." I encourage us to all be men of prayer as God awaits our call. Remember, the Father delights in the prayers of His saints.

As you do pray, please lift up Nancy and I, our family, One-on-One Ministries, driving folks on the shuttle van, our work at the church at Gaffney where I am now the interim pastor, and some of our practical living situations. Also, please allow me to pray for any needs you might have. So, that is my question for you this month: *"What are some of your needs? How can I be praying for you?"*

I love you, my dear friends.

Your friend,
Lee

Question: "Why is it so important to address a person by name? Why is it that one's name is so significant?"

Answer: "When I hear someone address me by name, it lets me know that they are making an effort to know me and that they care. Of course, in olden days and in the Bible, a name means much more than it does today. Each name actually meant something about them, their character, their family, etc. With your reminder, I would like to be more proactive in speaking to people by name." (RB)

Answer: "A name is one's own possession of identity. It is almost always the first intimate detail about yourself that you give to others. I think this is why 'it is so important to address a person by name.' Remembering someone's name shows you value their identity. I attended Bryan College, a Christian liberal arts college in Tennessee. My first days on campus as a freshman, the president of the college, Dr. Bill Brown, passed me in the hallway and called me by name; we had not met before. He had memorized all 300 freshman names and faces before they arrived. From that moment, I knew the president of Bryan College cared about me. We had a connection that was used to build a relationship. To this day, I remember the genuine feeling of respect I had, having my identity be valued by the president. I am still very impressed by this gesture. Placing value on one's identity by caring enough to call them by name opens the door for mutual respect, and the opportunity to reciprocate your own identity in Christ." (MM)

Answer: "The importance of calling someone by their proper name, I believe, implies a type of 'intimate,' relationship; it shows the person that you respect them. Why is a person's name important? I know that from the earliest records/history that we have available to us today—we also see this in the Bible—a person's name represents or implies a certain character trait." (KJ)

TO: My Dear Friends Whom I Call: "THE TABLE OF TWELVE" (January 2007)

Greetings! I hope this letter finds you and your families doing well. I also hope you had joyous time over Christmas and that your New Year is now starting out with some great possibilities.

Have you ever thought about Jesus and the many ways he went about evangelism and discipleship? Recently, one came to mind which I want to share because I feel it is fun, easy, and one all of us can do. I hope that I've got your attention and that you're on the edge of your seat. So, here goes.

I am ministering as an interim pastor in a small town about 45 minutes north of Greenville. The particular area of this little church is located in is a rough, depressed village where the mills were closed several years ago. Many of the people either do not have jobs, or they are working for low wages wherever jobs can be found. Also, there are many drug- and alcohol-related problems, and most barely make it from week to week. I guess you now have an idea of the conditions.

Anyway, shortly after I took this position, the church had its yearly Homecoming Service. This is a service that celebrates the past. Many previous members, family, and friends come to join in this joyous occasion. On this particular day, our little church of 20-30 had close to 100 people come and later stayed for dinner afterwards. What a thrill it was to hear singing fill this little church, to have an opportunity to see relationships grow, and to have the Gospel preached.

A few weeks later, when discussing how to evangelize our community for Christ with one of the elders, we both noted how God moved on many people to come for the Homecoming Service. When we summarized why, I knew the folks did not really come to sing or hear my preaching (even though they did enjoy the singing and put up with the preacher). Nonetheless, the real reason was to enjoy the food and then to fellowship with one another.

It then hit both of us. Why not have more times of eating and fellowship? The seed was planted. I went home and later looked at the life of Jesus and found it to be a common way he often got with people and shared the gospel of His heart. He was even known as one who "eats with publicans and sinners." Later, the disciples, who followed his lead, were asked, "Why do you eat with the uncircumcised?"

I then asked, "Why is eating so important for evangelism and discipleship?" (Good question, huh? Well, maybe.) When we eat at the same table, it brings all parties together as each has the same thing in common: the food. From this initial union, conversations can then springboard into other areas. Have you ever wondered why we refer to the Lord's Table as "Communion?" It is for the shear fact that we share the body (bread) and blood (wine) of our Lord in common, and this unites us in Christ; thus, *Common-Union*, "COMMUNION." Interesting, huh?

So, why do I share this, my friends on the Table of Twelve? Because it is something we can all do. Simply ask a person out to eat, go, and become their friend. Who knows? Maybe it will one day be said, "You eat with people you'd never catch me eating with." And then we can respond, "It never seemed to bother my Lord, and it doesn't bother me. By the way, are you hungry?" Now, let's get something to eat!

Your friend,
Lee

P.S. We're meeting again with others to eat this Sunday for a New Year's Celebration. Pray for us.

TO: My Dear Friends Whom I Call: "THE TABLE OF TWELVE" (February 2007)

It's cold in these here parts of South Carolina. What happened to those 70-degree temperatures we were experiencing two weeks ago? I must admit, I got spoiled. How are you and yours? How are things going? Please do keep me updated about your lives and happenings.

I did so appreciate the responses I received from some of you about using meals as a means for friendships, discipleship, and evangelism. I wanted to encourage you each with what one person shared last month:

> I continue to appreciate your letters. My wife and I joking call what you discuss the 'Ministry of Food.' We are constantly feeding college students in our home, an actual budget item in our family budget. I'd say three times a week there are three or more college students over at our place... it is a great opportunity for them to get some of Renae's excellent cooking and for us to fellowship, learn about their lives, and be invited to be involved when they have needs. Our girls have learned to accept this as a normal part of life, and it makes it easy to find babysitters when needed. ☺ (M/M)

I do so hope you all will try and ask someone out to eat this month. Just sit down, and get to know them. That's all it takes. And who knows what God might do one-on-one as you make a new friend.

Attached to this month's letter is the first half of a book I have been working on for the last 15 months. It is getting near the publication stage. In it, I teach about One-on-One relationships in action and through suggestion. You will be some of my first readers if you so desire to read "Signal." My prayers are with you.

Your friend,
Lee

TO: My Dear Friends Whom I Call: "THE TABLE OF TWELVE" (March 2007)

Greetings! As always, I hope this letter finds you and your families all doing well. We are excited here as the warm weather starts to approach, and new activities are seen on the horizon.

Adam is in his sophomore year at Anderson University, Christina is a freshman at Charleston Southern, Hannah is a junior in high school, Rebecca is in the sixth grade, and Sarah finishing up her second grade year at a special school for dyslexic students. Nancy is teaching preschool, and I am an interim pastor in Gaffney, SC on weekends.

During the week, I drive a shuttle van for an automotive research facility (Timken) and have found multiple opportunities to engage in one-on-one ministry relationships.

For instance, a supervisor came to me and asked for my help on several occasions concerning his future.

A security guard called me into the furnace room recently and began crying as he shared some of the problems in his life.

An engineer and I have been meeting weekly for Bible Study in one of the conference rooms at lunchtime.

Three Atheists have engaged me on an online debate concerning God's existence, old/young earth, and evolution/creation.

A mathematician talks with me regularly about his life and his strained marriage.

A Christian brother prays for me whenever I ask.

The list could go on and on, but what I am trying to convey is that God is developing many of these kinds of one-on-one ministry relationships.

One gentleman from work wrote me a note this week saying,

> I just wanted to be the first person to give a praise report. My God is such an awesome God... I have said all that to say this: without your guidance and prayer, I would still be roaming in the dark... I can't tell you enough how that little prayer and those few words of encouragement helped this wondering soul. I mean this from the depths of my soul. Lee, I love you...

Did not Jesus say, "The fields are white unto harvest, but the laborers are few. Pray ye therefore, the Lord of the harvest, that he might send forth laborers into his harvest fields."

I try to pray for each of you regularly for various things in your lives that you have mentioned in the past, but also that God might develop one-on-one ministry relationships with those with whom you have regular contact.

Please pray for me, too, as this ministry continues to grow. Also, pray for my job situation as the shuttle van position will be ending next week, and I am looking to fill a chaplain's position within the context of a company or corporation in our area.

Be encouraged, my dear friends. God has some great things in store. What is past is past, and new horizons lay before us. May you go with God grace and his blessings.

Your friend,
Lee

TO: My Dear Friends Whom I Call: "THE TABLE OF TWELVE" (April 2007)

He came up to me the other day at work. I could sense he wanted to talk. I needed to listen. *"Lee, I think God may be calling me to the ministry. I used to be on the corporate ladder. Not anymore. I really am considering this. What do you think?"* He is my boss at the place I work. And that was last week.

Often, I am confronted with people daily who just want to share their lives. Recently, I took a training course with Marketplace Chaplains USA. (At present, they have 2,000 chaplains placed in businesses all over America.) In their training, they stated that God has divine appointments awaiting us every day if we will just look for them.

I have since taken them at their word, and I have found this to be true. Now, it seems as though a day does not pass without encountering someone whom God has put in my path to minister His grace. As I start the days now, I look forward to the next appointment.

I echo the words of our Lord: *"The fields are white unto harvest."* I do this to encourage you, my dear friends. Opportunity is overflowing if we will only look for it!

I pray for you regularly that you will have one-on-one relationships with other people. From my studies in Scripture, Jesus spent more one-on-one time with others than anything else, more one-on-one time than with large crowds or small groups.

The need for one-on-one ministries in our lives is vital for the propagation of God's Kingdom on this earth and for the ministry of the gospel. I am therefore asking you, my friends, to pray and ask God to develop one-on-one relationships with those you encounter in your daily lives.

I hadn't really talked to her before. She worked at the other end of the building. I was down that way, so I stopped and reintroduced myself. I asked her if she had any children and if she was married. She didn't, and she wasn't. Eventually, our conversation led to her dating life. Do you have boyfriend?

"No," she replied, "but I do have a girlfriend."

For a moment, I was caught off guard. "Oh, I see. So, you live that kind of lifestyle. Okay, I just don't run into that very often." She smiled and we talked some more.

God has laid it on my heart to be her friend. Jesus was a friend to sinners. You never know who your next divine appointment may encounter. My prayers are with you.

Your friend,
Lee

P.S. One-on-One Ministries is growing. Please keep this type of ministry active in your own lives and in your prayers.

TO: My Dear Friends Whom I Call: "THE TABLE OF TWELVE" (May 2007)

Martin Luther, I am told, thought very highly of the printed page and used it countless times in propagating and sharing the message of Jesus Christ. Have you ever considered the multitude of ways that we have to do the same?

I have been exploring different ways in which to share my faith over the last couple of years. For example, my monthly letters to you, cards, the publication of my book, notes to people who need encouragement, etc. There is something special about a word rightly fashioned. As Solomon says, "It is like apples of gold in pictures of silver."

Recently, I was disturbed by how our Greenville community and some churches treat smokers. After much thought and deliberation, I decided to write to the newspaper in our town. So far, I've been pleased with the response, and it has given me a chance to share my faith. I would like to share that letter with you today:

April 28, 2007

Dear Editor,

I am a pastor in a conservative evangelical denomination with over thirty years of ministry experience. What I am about to say may shock some, but I feel it needs to be said. It concerns the issue of smokers in our society and the treatment they receive by many non-smokers.

Let me begin by saying, I am not a smoker, nor do I plan on smoking and frankly do not really care to be around others when they are smoking. Nonetheless, I cannot negate the fact that smokers are people, and people need to be treated with value.

Today's smokers are receiving the same type of treatment history once attributed to leprosy. They are told they can't smoke here, there, or just about anywhere. So, we see them standing in the rain, the cold, beside garbage bins, and in the backs of buildings as though they possess some type of hideous disease.

When I was younger and reports of smoking were just coming to the surface, we still treated smokers with respect. In the schools, they were given a smoking lounge. In restaurants, there was a place for smokers. Smokers were treated as human beings with value, honor, and dignity.

It pains me today to see how one portion of our society now treats others who are created in the image of God. Granted, I know smoking is detrimental to one's health. But so is overeating, drinking, the lack of exercise, etc.

Is what we are seeing a modern day form of leprosy? I simply pose the question and leave you with the answer. Let us treat *every human being with respect, honor, and dignity. I would welcome your response.*

Rev. Lee Moseley
Greenville, SC

Our Lord also used the printed page when He gave us the Bible. Consider using the printed page where you live. I leave this with you to think about, praying for you here as we minister together, one-on-one.

Your friend,
Lee

TO: My Dear Friends Whom I Call: "THE TABLE OF TWELVE" (June 2007)

Last month, I was pleased to get some good comments on my article in our Greenville newspaper. Bigger than the article I wrote was the fact that I saw the importance of the printed page as a strong vehicle in communication. With God's help, I hope to use it more in the future to share, minister, and expose the gospel as God gives me opportunity.

This month marks a historic moment in the life of One-On-One Ministries. It was one year ago that I sat across the table from Jim Pearce as he challenged me to begin this work. I could never have believed God would work in my life by working with men while doing something I so enjoyed. (You never know when what you say to someone might have such a great impact on them and on the lives of many others – thanks Jim!)

Two weeks ago in Irmo, SC, One-On-One Ministries became incorporated as a non-profit corporation when we officially had our first board meeting. I was greatly assisted in this venture by my old friend, Robby Buck, and a new friend named Greg Bushorr.

This past year, I have seen God minister to countless men, one-on-one—locally, nationally and internationally. Meeting with men and trying to serve them with the gospel of God's grace has been a blessing. Often, we engage such topics as God, salvation, marriage, jobs, suicide, children, emotional upheaval, insecurity, pornography, drugs, relationships, etc.

In the near future, we are hoping to acquire our 501(c)(3) non-profit corporation status from the IRS. I am truly excited and appreciative to our Lord for what He is doing and the opportunity to be a part of this ministry. Please continue to keep us in your prayers.

Over and over, God has continued to confirm this much-needed outreach. We all seem to speak of large churches and small group ministries, but rarely do we speak of one-on-one encounters with others as a regular part of the believer's life. Yet, this is what Jesus was constantly about more than anything else he did in his ministry while on earth.

Recently, I have had to go to a new chiropractor for some spinal problems. In my last visit, I found out from his wife that their son (and only child) committed suicide 16 years ago. Today, he opened up a little more with me about himself. Pray for Ray as I attempt to be there for him and become his friend.

In closing, I cannot thank each of you enough for your prayers and encouragement over this past year. As we enter these next 12 months, I ask you not only to pray for this ministry but to also stay close to me with your friendship and encouragement. *The Table of Twelve* has been a source of strength to me this past year, more than you know.

I pray for each of you and your families on a regular basis. You know I am here for you as I know you are for me. May God use each of us as we enter our daily lives, encountering others, one-on-one, for His honor and glory. From my heart, I thank each and every one of you for your friendship.

Your friend,
Lee

TO: My Dear Friends Whom I Call: "THE TABLE OF TWELVE" (July 2007)

Have you ever had one of those moments when things have been fun but very painful at the same time? That's right, "Fun and Painful." Over the last month, I have laughed with God and also went through some of the most chronic and severe physical pain I have ever experienced.

Concerning the laughter, I was reading about Abraham, who was *a friend of God*. In Genesis 17, we find he actually laughed *with* (not at) God over the word of Sarah having a baby in their old ages. God also had me laughing with Him one day in my car about what He is doing in my life. He really tickles me sometimes at the things He does. How about you? Do you ever laugh with God? Try it sometimes. It's fun!

Then, there is the pulled muscle in my neck. The pain has been awful. Little did I consider, God was up to something again. Have you ever thought about how God can use pain for our good and for His glory?

After much suffering, I finally went to see my new chiropractic doctor and then to a therapist. In the process, I was able to minister God's grace in unusual way. The doctor's wife got involved in a conversation we were having and shared an in-depth story about their 11-year-old son (their only child) who committed suicide. What an honor to be there to hear this dear woman share the deepest story of their lives.

Later, I had the opportunity to assist my therapist as she shared of starting a Special Needs Christian School in our area. I never would have thought my painful neck would be used so much by God.

Then, yesterday, I was walking in my neighborhood when a police officer pulled up next to me. He'd just been given our area to patrol. We talked. His name is Sam, and it seemed as though he and I hit it off immediately. He, too, shared some of his life with me. The fields are truly white unto harvest, aren't they?

As for the ministry here, One-on-One Ministries is now incorporated as I await the 501(c)(3) non-profit status from the IRS. One among our "Table of Twelve" put up the needed monies to see this incorporation come to fruition. How exciting it is to see God slowly moving us along! I pray regularly for each of you, your families, and your personal requests. I also pray God is developing one-on-one relationships in your lives.

Next month, I plan on enlarging "The Table of Twelve" to others who seem to be showing an interest in this ministry. Even though this is true, each of you will still and always be considered my core group, and I will continue to stay in touch with you as you mean so much to me.

I am also looking to develop this ministry in areas that will require funding. I am asking that each of my friends on "The Table of Twelve" will consider supporting me and One-on-One Ministries over the next year at whatever amount you feel led.

I truly believe what God exposed to my heart over a year ago is something He planned in my life before eternity began. I have a burning desire to see multitudes of people sitting together, One-on-One, as God establishes His presence in their midst.

As I close, I would like you to consider three things:

1) Pray that God would restore his presence among his people as Jesus did when He walked upon this earth in those special one-on-one relationships;

2) Pray about supporting One-on-One Ministries over the next twelve months; and
3) Try spending time laughing with God this month. It's really a lot of fun! God wanted me to tell you that.

Your Friend,
Lee

TO: My Dear Friends Whom I Call: "THE TABLE OF TWELVE" (August 2007)

If you are receiving this communiqué, you are part of an elite group called, "The Table of Twelve." This group was organized last year to help in the foundational stages of One-on-One Ministries. As a part of this elite and growing work, One-on-One Ministries is going to be sending you a monthly newsletter, encouraging you in your Christian walk and ministry.

So, what is One-on-One Ministries? In a nutshell, it is a ministry that encourages men to meet individually with other men in order to be their friends and to help encourage their lives. In the process of meeting with others in one-on-one relationships, doors of ministry begin to open as we fulfill our Lord's example as being a friend to others (sinners).

We truly believe that One-on-One Ministries holds the number one pattern of ministry our Lord was most active in modeling. Check it out. Look at each Gospel book while making three categories of how Jesus spent his time ministering: 1) large groups, 2) small groups, and 3) one-on-one encounters. You may be shocked to see that Jesus spent more of his time in one-on-one encounters than in any other thing he did. That is not to say the other things are not also important, but it is to recognize that if He spent most of his time in this arena, should we not also?

Yesterday, I stopped by McDonald's for a biscuit. When I went to get a napkin, I noticed a local attorney whom I had not seen in a while. I tapped him on the shoulder to say, "Hello." The next thing you know, we were engaged in a two-hour conversation.

I have found that these divine appointments from God are everywhere if we will just look for them. I challenge you to ask the Lord to give you a divine appointment tomorrow. It might just surprise you who God will bring your way. Honest! Pray for that today, my friend!

As for a word of personal encouragement, have you ever thought of God laughing with you? He laughed with Abraham whom he called his friend. Have you ever thought about God singing with you? In Zephaniah, the prophet says, "He dances over us with singing." If that is true, then God dances with us, too! Sounds like God likes to have a lot of fun with us. Think about it. He also wants to have fun with you. Why? Because he loves you!

Another word of encouragement: We have always taken, hookline-and-sinker, the saying, "Obedience brings blessings." Have you ever considered that might be wrong? I had not until someone challenged me recently. Instead, let's consider, "Blessings bring obedience."

What came first: the blessing of Creation or God's requirement to be obedient?

What came first: the blessing of the Cross or repentance/faith?

What came first in all of Paul's Epistles: the indicatives or the imperatives? (Paul seems to share the blessings we have in Christ before telling us how we are to live our lives.) Interesting, huh? I've found it revolutionary!

Well, that's about all God had for me to share with you today. Welcome aboard the One-on-One Ministries' Table of Twelve. We've got a feast in store and a long trip ahead of us. So, sit back, relax, and hold on tight. Our journey is just about to get very exciting.

Your friend,
Lee

Clarifications on the August Communiqué

In my last letter, I did not mean to give the impression that men always needed to initiate contacts with other men in order for one-on-one relationships to work. To clarify, if that were true, then most of us would feel totally out of place. I do believe such relationships do occur from time to time, but more often, I have found that God initiates our one-on-one contacts for us throughout the day in ways that come by natural means.

For instance, someone may come up to me and begin a conversation at the water fountain, or a friend may come by to talk, or I may run into someone I have not seen in a while. In each of these cases and in others, I pray ahead of time and believe God sets them up as "divine appointments," whether it is to have a listening ear, to say a kind word of encouragement, or to offer some insight or counsel. Sometimes, it is just to let God minister to me through this person he has brought my way. At other times, we minister to each other.

Sometimes, these relationships move into deeper friendships. Other times, God only sets the appointment for just that moment. In either case, I try to see these as God's divine appointments for the time being. I also seem to leave the moment praying for the other individual, believing God had us meet at this time for His glory.

Another area of clarification involves the question, "Does *obedience bring blessings* or should it be that *blessings bring obedience?*" I would not go so far as to say obedience does not bring blessings, but I cannot help but believe the intent of Scripture moves us to think this way as all blessings originate in and from God.

For instance, in the Old Testament, God tells the children of Israel they have forgotten and forsaken (disobeyed) the Lord their God who brought them out of Egypt. Here, the reflection of their obedience was then to be on the *Lord God who brought them out of Egypt* (the blessing). As we look at the Bible, the blessings always seem to precede the obedience.

Let me give you a practical illustration. One day, Nancy and I got into a big argument on the way to the dentist. I was convinced I was right and that she was wrong. (I even told her so; big mistake!) Then, I asked God to show me what He had been teaching me. Over a short period of time, I soon began to focus on this precious gift (my wife) God had given me and how I was treating her in this matter. When I started to see the blessing of my beautiful prize (Nancy), my heart broke, and I soon found myself repentant of the way I was treating her.

Anyway, I found myself apologizing to both God and Nancy. It was also interesting that God had been dealing with her, too. In a moment of time, our walls of defense came down, unity was brought back to the Moseley marriage, and God was glorified in the moment. So, you can observe how seeing God's blessing brought about the proper obedience that, in turn, brought peace to our home and honored God in the process.

Rejoicing here,
Lee!

TO: My Dear Friends Whom I Call: "THE TABLE OF TWELVE" (September 2007)

Divine opportunities are everywhere.

He was folding a huge black tarp in his front yard as I was passing by on my daily walk through the neighborhood. He had only one good arm. I stopped, walked over, and said, "Let me help you." Five minutes later, I had formed a new relationship with Jimmy. After shaking his hand and heading down the street, I prayed for my new friend. I'm looking forward to seeing Jimmy again.

Divine appointments are everywhere.

I prayed, "Lord, would you please bless One-on-One Ministries?"

A few minutes later, the phone rang. It was Charlie, an Anglican Minister in Greenville. "Lee, I'd like to do an outreach conference in Greenville at the end of October, and I'd like for you to be the keynote speaker." God is good!

Divine appointments are everywhere.

Today, I decided to take my walk early as I had a meeting tonight. I hadn't been out the door 10 minutes when an elderly gentleman spoke to me as he was moving his trashcan to the garage from the street. I stopped. We talked about the trash, where I lived, and the city government. I introduced myself, and Mr. Mann did likewise. I departed. I now have another new relationship in the neighborhood. "Thank you Lord for giving me this acquaintance with Mr. Mann."

Divine appointments are everywhere.

An email came from a friend:

Thanks for thinking of me. You are so right about what a force we can be by simply reaching out to other men, one-at-a-time. I have been meeting with a friend one-on-one for two years now, weekly, and from this, we have started our small men's group at church. Now, we have 10-12 men trying to take our group to the next step, reaching men one-on-one. Maybe we could have lunch soon and share some thoughts.

Divine appointments are everywhere.

I wanted to start my walk early. The sun seems to be setting sooner each evening. One house down, I saw Mark. He turned off his riding lawnmower, and I knew it was time to talk. Divine appointments can often change our schedules. Mark told me he was moving to Barbados for three years on a new job assignment. I hope that we'll talk some more before he leaves next week. Interesting, isn't it? I now will know somebody in Barbados. Who knows what God has in store?

I left Mark. The time was getting late. Forget being home before the sun sets. As a matter of fact, it would be dark by the time I arrived. I'd been asking God recently how he danced over me. As I was finishing my walk, He surprised me. A little star was twinkling in the distance and dancing in the great expanse of space. He gave me an appointment with Mark so I could have an appointment with Him. He had answered my prayer. He wanted to show me how much He loved me.

Divine appointments are everywhere.

You just have to be looking for them. I truly believe God wanted me to tell you that.

Your friend,
Lee

TO: My Dear Friends Whom I Call: "THE TABLE OF TWELVE" (October 2007)

Greetings! When you hear the word, *evangelism*, what do you think? "Great for others but not for me." Why? Because it scares us and often seems so unnatural and stiff. Right? "Yes." But suppose I could show you how to make evangelism a natural part of life and fun at the same time. Would you listen? I think so. Let me begin then with a story of four frogs. I think you'll like it.

Two frogs came upon two other frogs that fell into a deep hole. As the two tried to jump out, they did nothing but bump and cut themselves up against the walls of the hole. When the two at the top saw their futile pursuits, they began yelling, screaming, and waving their little arms, saying, "Stop! You're only going to hurt yourselves! Stop!" Finally, one stopped, curled up, and died. But the other continued jumping and finally jumped out of the hole.

In their amazement, they came over to the little frog, got face-to-face with him, and asked, "How did you do it? How did you make it out of that hole?"

He replied, "Fellows, you see, I am deaf, and when I saw you cheering, that gave me the motivation and encouragement I needed to jump out of the hole." You see, one's perception worked for the bad while the other's worked for the good.

Often our perception of evangelism is the same. Our understanding of evangelism has been dulled. This is what One-on-One Ministries is trying to change in the lives of men as our purpose is this: "To engage men in friendly, one-on-one relationships with the gospel of Jesus Christ in order to help and strengthen their lives for the glory of God and His Kingdom."

How do we change our perception? To start, we first must look at the life of Christ and observe the example He passed on to those around him. What did he do, and what did he model?

We talk of Jesus often as being Prophet, Priest, and King, but how often do we see him in the light of the Gospels as being a *Friend*? Jesus, throughout his life's ministry, was known as a "friend to sinners." Have you ever seen evangelism in this light, that of being a friend? That's it!

Our primary focus is to teach men how to befriend other men. As we initiate these relationships, we then move into new dynamics with them. We, who are Christians, carry with us God's presence and cannot help but to exude the light of Christ. This eventually moves our friendships to natural conversations that progress into discussions about our Lord. Sometimes, God opens these discussions up rather quickly. At other times, they take long periods of time.

What we are saying is this: "Jesus' model of evangelism was often befriending others." This, too, has become our theme at One-on-One Ministries, learning just to "be a friend."

I'll leave you with that to ponder, and I will share more next time. I am also including an addendum on "The Power of One" that I thought you might like. Meanwhile, try simply to "be a friend" as our Lord was "a friend to sinners." These are some things I just felt He wanted you to know. By the way, last night on my walk, he appeared out of nowhere. "Hi," I said.

"Hey," he replied. "I see you walking everyday."

We introduced ourselves. His name was Joel. We walked together for a while and talked. Joel shared of his faith in Christ. As we parted, I asked him if I could pray for him about anything. I also asked if he'd pray for me. He told me he would and that he prayed for me last night when he saw me out walking.

Later, I thanked God for Joel. To think that God has others I sometimes am not even aware of, praying for me. That was such an encouragement. My dear friends, I hope these words encourage you. I, too, am praying for you regularly.

Your friend,
Lee
"The Power of One"

It's just amazing how one person can impact so many others. Did you know that Jesus was constantly making one-on-one impacts? Jesus was definitely interested in others. In Matthew, he had 25 one-on-one encounters with others; in Mark, 21; in Luke, 26; and in John, 27. He literally had 99 (based on my findings) recorded. If Jesus thought it was so important, shouldn't we? I think we should.

In the Gospels, Jesus asked 237 questions to others. In Jesus' day, learning to frame the proper question often had more impact than giving the proper answer. It's true; questions often get right to one's heart and life. Imagine that.

Have you ever considered the power of one?

My retired mom visits our church now and then. A few months ago, she started bringing Bibles and giving them out to those who either wanted one or did not have one. She would pick these up during the week at no cost from thrift stores that give them away free. She started giving away Bibles to anyone who wanted one for their own use or to pass on to another person. Soon, I started doing the same thing. During our VBS (Vacation Bible School), I gave Bibles to all the children attending. It was not long before Bibles were made available as an ongoing part of our church.

One Sunday, we accumulated so many Bibles that a Bible was given to each person attending, and they were asked to keep it for themselves or to pass it on to another person. Recently, we even put a sign up in front of our church that said, "Every Sunday, Free Bibles." Last week, I noticed our supply of Bibles diminished. Then, on Sunday morning, an amazing thing happened. It seemed unusual and unexpected at the same time. When our elder arrived at the church to open the doors, he found two bags filled with 10 brand new Bibles, sitting outside the door. There was no note or anything. Apparently, someone in the community saw the sign and just wanted to be a part of our ministry. I wrote a letter to the local paper, sharing this story. Saturday, I received a note from the editor saying they were going to publish it.

Have you ever consider the power of one?

I recently saw an old picture of a preacher sharing a Bible story to a group of children, sitting on the edge of a ditch back in the Forties. I've been wanting to reach the people in our area for a while, but I just hadn't known how. In bed one Tuesday night, God gave me a similar idea. The next day, I went to the home of a child who had visited our Vacation Bible School this summer.

Upon arriving, I asked Brittney to go get some friends, and I would tell them a story. When she returned, no one was with her. "Okay Lord," I said to myself and then proceeded. Her mother sat on the porch and, later, her aunt joined us. I told of David slaying the great giant, Goliath. Although I spoke to the girl, I could tell I also had the adults' attention. I concluded by sharing the gospel of God's care and protection. I then had prayer and told Brittney I'd be back every week to tell her and any friends a Bible story. She seemed delighted (and so did the adults). Could God use this one little girl to reach our area? Who knows?

Have you ever considered the power of one?

Did you know that if the Christians in America alone would reach just one new friend a year and then get that friend to do likewise the next year, we could reach everyone on earth with the gospel in just five years? Just one person per year! That's all.

Have you ever considered the power of one?

Oh well, so much for numbers. But I do feel God wanted me to share that with you. Maybe you are that one to start it all.

Have you ever considered the power of one?

Your friend,
Lee

TO: My Dear Friends Whom I Call: "THE TABLE OF TWELVE" (November 2007)

Greetings, dear friends! I hope this letter finds you all doing well, prospering and in good health. It's now Thanksgiving time again, a time for family, food, and festivities. It's a time to reflect on the things God has done for us this year. It's a time to remember our heritage from whence we came.

In 1623, Governor William Bradford of Plymouth Colony gave the first Thanksgiving Proclamation:

Inasmuch as the Great Father's given us this year an abundant harvest... has granted us freedom to wor-

ship God according to the dictates of our own con-
science... I, your magistrate, do proclaim that all ye
Pilgrims, with your wives & ye little ones, do gather at
ye meeting house, on ye hill... there to listen to ye pastor & render thanksgiving to ye Almighty God for all
his blessings.

In 1776, George Washington and his troops, moving
close to Valley Forge, deliberately stopped in bitter weather
in the open fields to celebrate Thanksgiving. George Washington, a few months after his inauguration, issued
"Presidential Proclamation Number One." In it, President
Washington stated,

It is the duty of all Nations to acknowledge the provi-
dence of Almighty God.

In 1863, President Lincoln issued a proclamation, setting aside the last Thursday in November as the day of
national Thanksgiving. Lincoln restored the neglected
presidential proclamations of prayer and thanksgiving
during the Civil War:

Intoxicated with unbroken success, we have become
too self-sufficient to feel the necessity of redeeming
and reserving grace, too proud to pray to the God that
made us...

No president since Lincoln has forgotten Thanksgiving to God each year, weaving a picture of our most beloved tradition.

In 2007, what a glorious honor it is to be reminded of our heritage. Yet, what disturbs my heart is a statistic I recently heard. In America, every denomination is now in decline. Not one is growing. To my knowledge, not since the Civil War has our country experienced this happening. The faith of our forefathers is being lost. So, at this Thanksgiving time, I would like to offer up a prayer on behalf of our country to return to our heritage. Would you please join me as I offer this prayer?

O God, at this Thanksgiving time, forgive us for forsaking thee, the God of our fathers. May you now arrest our hearts and minds, bless us, and bring our families together again to serve thee? And may you continue to extend your blessings upon our great nation, guiding us one and all by your most holy Word? May you also grant us patience and perseverance in the unexpected tests and trials of life? May you impress upon us the spirit of our forefathers, their deep-soul cravings for you as we meet with the particular challenges of our days?

And now, may we, O God, be a people again who meet weekly in the house of God as families with our children, grandchildren, and great-grandchildren to worship and honor the Lord God Almighty? And let us always approach your throne, oh Heavenly Father, with true thankfulness - not just for today, but for every day, not only in triumphs, but also in trials - acknowledging our utter dependence on you to supply all our needs, for in you we live, and move, and have our being.

Therefore, let us choose this day whom we are going to serve. And may we go from here today saying as Joshua of old, 'But as for me and my house, we will serve the Lord.' To God be the glory. In the most holy Name of our Lord and Savior, Jesus Christ, do we pray. Amen.

Thank you.

Your friend,
Lee

One-On-One "Moseley" Update

November 23, 2007

Dear friends on "The Table of Twelve,"

I hope and pray you had a wonderful Thanksgiving. All of our children were at home. The biggest delight was to catch up and also observe what God is doing in each life. I can see these times will be rare, and oh, how I do miss them. It's hard to believe how fast the years pass, and then they are gone. But God is good; is he not? I see my children growing up, sometimes through hard means and other times through good ones. Nonetheless, my prayer is that they will follow him.

Adam will be 21 in January. He's a junior, studying mathematics with a desire for graduate school and then on to be a college professor. He is dating a nice Christian girl, named Grace, whom we all like. (Only time will tell of their future, so we try and stay out of the way.) Grace is teaching Adam some long overdue etiquette as we see our boy becoming a young man.

Christina (19) is a sophomore at Charleston Southern University, hoping to major in English as she has a talent for creative writing. She is taking next semester off to travel to Kenya where she will work at an orphanage and receive "Life Credits" toward her degree. We also feel God has some big lessons in store for our daughter while there. So, please pray for our Christina.

Hannah will be 18 in January and is a senior in high school. She's now planning to forego her life of sports and concentrate next year on her studies as she is looking at USC in Columbia. Hannah is 10 points away from getting a scholarship on her next SAT test. She is a good kid who causes no trouble but is our silent, mystery child. So, pray for her parents as we try and guide her.

Rebecca will be 13 in December and is a seventh-grader. She is an excellent student who has had a hard time developing relationships at her new school over the past year, but we have seen how God answers prayer as she cried when we discussed this over dinner. She is such a delight and realizes now that God's plan has been to deepen friendships through a very long process.

Sarah (9) is a third-grader in a "special needs school" for dyslexia. She is doing well and may be ready next year to return to "traditional schooling." All love Sarah as she is a servant and friend to all she meets. Two teachers from her last school two years ago say they still talk of Sarah and how unique she was and how they miss her. She sees nothing but goodness in others.

Nancy works part-time in a preschool with three-year-olds and loves it. Two nights a week, she works at Stein Mart where she is redesigning our wardrobes with her great discounts. Nancy loves being a Mom, and when she's not, she loves serving others. Our house is a home because Nancy makes it that way. She gives and gives and gives. I sometimes worry she gives too much.

Lee (that's me). I have three things going right now: 1) I pastor part-time at a church 45 miles north of here in Gaffney, SC; 2) I have written two books that will hopefully soon be published; and 3) One-on-One is growing as we now have over 50 people on our mailing list and the possibility of several conferences in 2008. My deepest delight is walking with the Lord while enjoying him, my family, and the work he has called me to do. I covet each of your prayers.

Finally, I have been asked how my first conference went two weeks ago. As far as I can tell, things went great. I talked with the pastor recently, and he said it was just what they needed. I had a few kinks but nothing anyone would notice. So, overall, for my first conference, it went well. Thanks so much for your prayer support and interest. This meant more to me than you know. You're a group of very special people. Continue having a wonderful holiday season in His honor.

Your friend,
Lee

TO: My Dear Friends Whom I Call: "THE TABLE OF TWELVE" (December 2007)

Season's greetings! I am told the first Christmas tree came in response to Martin Luther. He cut down a tree in the countryside, brought it home, and placed candles on it for all to see and be reminded that Christ is the light of the world. That is how I'm told we got our first Christmas tree.

Speaking of Luther's life, he also preached strongly of man's lost condition and his need for Christ. I never questioned this logic until a professor of mine said Calvin approached his preaching totally different from Luther. Whereas Luther's focus was on man and his need, Calvin's was on God and his greatness, thus exposing man to "the Light."

As I have pondered these two approaches, I have slowly begun to embrace Calvin's view. When people see Christ in us, both in word and deed, their lives are exposed. They either run from the light, or they are drawn to it in hopes of receiving the help they need: Christ.

"So, what in the world does that have to do with Christ, Christmas, and One-on-One Ministries?"

Well I'm glad you asked, and since you did, I'll try to answer your question.

Jesus was a friend to sinners. Throughout his life, he was known as being strong in word and deed. When encountering others one-on-one, he did not go in with his pistols blazing, ready to cut them down. No! He went in to reveal His Father. As some encountered "the Light," they rebelled while others, when they saw their condition, came running for help.

What bothers me today is so many Christians lambasting the "evils" of Christmas. They talk of materialism, paganism, traditionalism, etc. But have we ever considered when we constantly elevate these "evils," our focus is on man? Granted, there are "evils," but I, too, think Calvin has a point in lifting up Christ, thus exposing those in need to "the Light."

"So, how do I make this happen in my life?"

By simply doing what Jesus did. And that comes by loving others and being their friend both with our words and actions. People are hurting. During the holidays, more people commit suicide than all the rest of the year combined. People are in desperate need of "the Light" of our Lord as he emanates from our lives.

I put him on the bus yesterday for Chicago. We met in the ninth grade, joined the Army together, and stayed in contact over the years. Sunday night, the phone rang. It was my old and dear friend, Mike. "Lee, I need your help. Can you help me?" Mike had finally come to the end of himself after 35 years of a drug-infested life.

Over the years, I've just tried to love Mike and be his friend. Often, it was very hard. Sometimes, I even wondered if my prayers would ever be answered. Then, the phone rang; it was Mike: "Lee, I need your help. Can you help me?"

The 'Light' had finally dawned. That is what Christmas is about: "the Light." I just thought He wanted me to tell you that.

Your friend,
Lee

P.S. Please do stay in touch as I love hearing from you!

TO: My Dear Friends Whom I Call: "THE TABLE OF TWELVE" (January 2008)

Yesterday, I went to our church to change the holiday sign. "Lord, what can I put up as we start this New Year?" I prayed.

Then, it came to me: "God loves to laugh, sing, and dance. Do you?" These were things I had glimpses of Him doing in 2007. "Why not?"

Tonight, I told Nancy I needed to be alone. Nothing soothes my heart more than to go on a walk with God. No phones, no chatter, and no TV; nothing in the background to disturb my Lord and me. The temperature was right with a light coat and a beautiful starlit sky. What more could I want or ask? It was just He and I walking together as friends in our usual way.

One-on-One Ministries is about friends. It's about developing friendships with those God brings across our paths of life. Have you ever considered that you are God's friend, and He is yours? Yes, we see Jesus befriending others as he was known to do, being a friend to sinners, (Luke 15:1-3). But have you ever considered your befriending Jesus?

That is what I did tonight. I just walked with Him as I normally do on these nighttime excursions. Our times are like that of friends. Some of the time, we talk, and I remind him of my problems as He shares with my heart how He is taking care of things. Some of the time is spent enjoying His presence and creation. He smiles and chuckles at my delight.

Sometimes, my mind wanders away, but His is always fixed on me. I told Him tonight, "I want to be with you, Lord."

He seemed to respond and say, "I want to be with you, Lee."

I was touched as I looked into the sky and embraced the silence of His presence. *What is man that you are mindful of him and the son of man that you visit him?* He loves me, you know; and He loves you. His eyes are forever fixed on us. That is wonderfully exciting!

Sometimes, I sing. Tonight, I did a little skip. That's okay for those who think I've lost it. So, what if I have? There is nothing that brings me greater joy than to be with my Father. God loves to laugh, sing, and dance. How about you? David danced before the Lord. Abraham laughed with God. Zephaniah says he sings over us. Now, Lee skips. Go figure!

Yes, Jesus was a friend who did things friends do with others. He laughed, sang, danced, and maybe even skipped, I suppose. He was constantly a friend to others. He also had many friends. At the end of His ministry, Scripture tells us he said to the disciples, "You are my friends" (John 15:14). Mighty words, aren't they?

To think, the disciples actually befriended Jesus. How about you? Have you thought about befriending Him? Adam did in the cool of the day. Moses on Mt. Sinai. David on the hillsides. The disciples each day in the Gospels. He so desires this more than we know!

This year, I want to encourage you to make a friend of Him by developing that friendship. It will be the greatest delight you will ever know or experience. Perhaps like me, you will one day find yourself walking with Him. Who knows? Maybe you'll even find yourself skipping with him.

Well, that is all from One-on-One Ministries as we begin 2008. Let us all remember, "God loves to laugh, sing, dance, (and possibly) skip." The question is, "Do we?" Just think about it. I really believe He wanted me to share that with you today.

Your friend,
Lee

TO: My Friends on "THE TABLE OF TWELVE"
(February 2008)

She sat, talking on her cell. I looked back one more time. My little girl had grown up. She was flying out to Kenya to live. "What's Dad to do? What happened to time? Could I have been a better father?" I made my mistakes; believe me. We all do; do we not? The questions swirled.

"But what about our times when riding together in the car as she shared her life, and I shared mine? How about the times we ate out and went to movies? And those sporting events Nancy and I craved seeing her involved in? And what about those late night talks?"

My heart broke but rejoiced, too. My little girl had grown up. She became a young lady before my eyes. Time passes so fast; does it not? Have you ever been there? I'm sure you have.

A few days later, I was talking with two men. One gentleman shared a Scripture from 2 Peter 2:13 to encourage the other man: "If we believe not, yet he abides faithful, he can not deny Himself." Little did these men realize, this Scripture was really meant for me.

Those words rushed over my soul as cool lotion to dry, hot skin. It was then that God started healing an area of my heart that so deeply needed His help. It did not all happen at once, but in that moment, he began to remind me that he is always faithful and can be trusted, whether with my life or my daughter's.

How about you? Do you ever experience moments when things get the best of you? When you don't seem to trust anymore? And you're not sure where life is going? Times you just feel like giving up but don't know where to go? I'm sure you do. I do. We all do.

I meet men all the time who are struggling with similar issues. Life seems to beat us up, and we wonder where God is or what is taking place? Life gets away from us. We can no longer hold on. The questions swirl. Then, we hear his soft words saying to us, "I abide faithful."

Why do I say this? Because we're alike, you and me. We need to hear His words and be reminded of His care. Others need to hear it, too. We need to share it with one another. We need to hear from heaven and be reminded of His faithfulness when ours is lacking.

Where are you today? Where is the person you are talking with at the water fountain or in the break room? Maybe they don't even need to hear it verbally. It just might be that they need to see us struggle with our faith and return to the words that our God is faithful still.

Many came saying, "Why are you letting your daughter go to Kenya, knowing the civil unrest the nation is experiencing?" I thought, "God, why are you asking this of me?" His words gave me rest as they continue to echo, "He abides faithful." Yes, He always does.

I've now come to terms with God on the matter. My faith has been tried and continues to be, but I am forever reminded of the goodness and greatness of my Father in whom I can trust even when I can't. Where are you today?

He truly does abide faithful. I just felt like He wanted me to share that with you.

Your friend,
Lee

TO: My Friends on "THE TABLE OF TWELVE"
(March 2008)

It's been 25 years since I first saw God move in my Christian life in such a miraculous way concerning friendships. I'd moved to Hilton Head, SC after college. The only person I knew was my mother.

After two months of work and then returning home each night, I was troubled. "Lord," I prayed, "I'm lonely. I don't know anyone, and I want some friends."

Three months later, I was the president of the Singles Group on Hilton Head Island and had more friends than you could imagine. So, what did God show me that caused all this?

I talk to men all the time regarding similar things. I feel most have many associates, but few have real friends. The reason: we, men, just don't know how to make it happen. Sure, we can talk business, news, or sports, but few of us have others to whom we can share our hearts.

Thom sat across the table. He'd been a friend for a very long time, one that had always been there for me and stood by my side in some troubling times of life. I was encouraging him to develop just one friendship this year. "Just one, Thom," I said. "Just one friend."

"How do I make friends? Lee, you say pray but how do I do it once God reveals that person or persons to me? How?" I could feel his loneliness and fear as I once remembered the past.

I could see I was leading a brother into a forest he'd never been. "Lee, that's easy for you to say! Why, you've never met a stranger. For me, it's a different story. Just be a friend? Don't you hear what I'm thinking? How in the world do I become someone else's friend? That's what I want to know? Just how do you do it? How? It is not that simple."

As I shared with Thom, my thoughts flashed back to the time on Hilton Head 25 years ago. I took him where God had taken me in my loneliness to the book of *Proverbs* where the Lord spoke through King Solomon, the wisest King who ever lived. He said, "If a man is to have friends, he must do this one thing: Do nothing more than be a friendly person" (Proverbs 18:24, my paraphrase).

I reflected on what God had called me to do. It was simply to be kind and considerate to others. It meant saying "hello," asking people about themselves, showing an interest in them, and being gracious and courteous. In essence, it was just showing God's love toward others, and thinking of creative ways to do it.

"So, Lee, it is just being cordial, huh?" I could sense he was pondering my words.

"That's right. It is just being a nice guy. I think anybody can do that; don't you?"

"So, Lee, you are saying it is just being friendly to all those you meet in your daily activities of life?" I could see the light had turned on, and Thom was now deep in thought.

"That's right, Thom. That's what I did 25 years ago, and I'm still doing it today. It's really easy and fun: 'HAVING FRIENDS COMES BY SIMPLY BEING FRIENDLY.'"

I just felt God wanted me to share that with you this month.

Your friend,
Lee

TO: My Dear Friends whom I call "THE TABLE OF TWELVE" (April 2008)

Greetings! I hope this letter finds you all doing well. I'm always encouraged each month when it is finally time to sit down and write to you. Last month, we talked of building friendships by simply stepping out and trying to be a friendly person (Proverbs 18:24). One friend, Jerry McKee, responded by saying,

> Thanks for sharing this with me. I agree with you 100%. I use this practice at work, and you can see results. I make it a habit to speak to everyone at one of our client's businesses (about 25 people) even if just to ask, "How are you doing?" I focus on the one person that everyone usually pushes aside to make them

feel special. Just to share with you one person, she was made to feel lonely by her work peers because she did not wear good clothes, and her hair was greasy looking, and she had a little odor about her. I make a point to talk to her and give a compliment about something she was doing. And now, she has a new hair-do and no odor, and she has made a lot of new friends. Sometimes, we have to lift people up, and you will see friends starting to come to you for that lift.

Thanks, Jerry. I, too, meet hurting people daily who just need a friendly face to offer a kind word in their pain. It is said that all of us are usually in one of three places at all times: we are either in the midst of suffering, entering suffering, or coming out of it. Even the Bible says, "As the sparks fly upward, man is born unto trouble" (Job 5:7), and "Man, who is born of women, is of few days, and full of trouble" (Job 14:1). Hurting people are everywhere; they just need a friend. Jesus was a friend to sinners.

Since last month, I spoke to Bill's wife, trying to console her over the loss of her husband.

Gary pulled me aside to share of his affair and divorce.

I called Steve yesterday morning to pray with him just before he was taken into surgery.

Last night, I shared good news with a child of mine who had been downcast over a certain situation.

Hurting people are everywhere; they just need a friend. Jesus was a friend to sinners.

Our Lord met her at a well and became her friend. She was hurting. She had been married five times, and the man she was now living with was not her husband.

Later, Jesus met a man living miserably in a graveyard setting. He, too, was hurting. He became his friend.

Zacchaeus was hated by all, for he was a tax collector. Few would have anything to do with him, yet Christ stopped by to have supper one evening.

Hurting people are everywhere; they just need a friend. Jesus was a friend to sinners.

They are all around. She sits in the cubicle as a single mom whose life is pushed to the limits.

His wife just left him for another man, and the house is now so quite without her it almost drives him crazy.

She's ugly, fat, and not very approachable. Yet, no one knows she is at the point of suicide. They are all calling out, "Will you be my friend?"

Hurting people are everywhere; they just need a friend. Jesus was a friend to sinners.

I just felt like God wanted me to share that with you today.

Your friend,
Lee

P.S. Also, I always enjoy hearing from each of you. Please do stay in touch, and let me how you are doing and what you think of the monthly letters. I always love to hear.